Use Your Words: How to Rapidly Grow Your Business with AI

AIPS Prompts, Volume 1

Bo Yoder

Published by Bo Yoder, 2023.

USE YOUR WORDS: HOW TO RAPIDLY GROW YOUR BUSINESS WITH AI

First edition. June 1, 2023.

ISBN: 979-8223596370

Written by Bo Yoder.

Table of Contents

This book is dedicated to Brian Roemelle, who has been building astonishing prompts and unique AI systems for decades. His generosity in sharing his wisdom online and in his Read Multiplex newsletter is what made me first take notice and say...I think it's time for me to pay attention to AI Large Language Models. Without the "ah-HA" moment he gave to me, this book would never have been written.

Introduction:
The Unlimited Power of Words

This book was NOT written by an Artificial Intelligence.

This book was also NOT written by a human being.

This book was written in a collaboration between the human and machine mind in a process best described as a "bottega workshop".

This master and apprentice model has been used by many of the world's great artists from antiquity to today.

In a bottega workshop, a master artist or craftsman will take on one or more apprentices who work in the master's workshop, learning the skills and techniques of the trade.

The apprentices typically begin by doing menial tasks, such as preparing canvases or mixing pigments, and then progress to more complex work under the guidance of the master.

The master acts as the designer and conductor, and ultimately has the final say in the creation of a masterpiece, often adding the finishing touches to a work that had been roughed out by an apprentice.

This model was common in Renaissance Italy and was used by many of the great artists of the period, including Michelangelo.

In more modern times, the glass artist Dale Chihuly lost an eye in a car accident in the 1970's, and this loss of depth perception made the already dangerous art of glass blowing impossible for him.

Rather than quitting his art, he built a collaborative team who execute the creation of all his works under his guidance.

This is exactly the process that works well when a human asks an AI to go to work for them.

The output from these systems can be astonishing, and can save many hours of effort, but sometimes the context is a bit off which can make the flow of a piece "feel weird" or there may be some glaring errors or false "facts" when the AI tries to fill in the blanks on something it has not been well trained on.

Just like a mechanized factory can crank out thousands of widgets per hour, there still needs to be some human oversight, "polishing" and quality control, in order that the finished product is truly ready to deliver to a client or audience.

At this point in my life, I have written two books that have been previously published in the traditional way by the major publishing house McGraw-Hill. ***"Mastering Futures Trading"*** and ***"Optimize Your Trading Edge"***.

Both these took more than a year to write.

The process was painful, and I never thought I would have the time and energy to write a book length manuscript again.

The book you are reading now which was written with a team of AI collaborators, using the "Bottega Model" took me just 23 DAYS to write.

That's the power of AI to accelerate your productivity and allow you to take on projects that otherwise wouldn't be possible for you.

I would estimate that 80% of the words in this book were written by me, but this time the process was painless because of all the help my

AI "assistants" gave me in the brainstorming, outlining, story arc and content list part of the writing process, which is where I spent the majority of my time in previous projects.

I have a busy life, working with clients as they learn a unique approach to forecasting financial market prices, and raising young children.

Time is my most precious currency by far.

Without AI, the bottega model and my AIPS concepts I'll share later on in this book...this would have been a multi-year project, and one quite frankly I never would have started.

Because of my AI "assistants", (who did all the grunt work) you now have something timely and tangible in your hands that I am excited to share with you.

I believe it can transform your life in so many positive ways, and I hope you follow through and DO THE WORK, so that you can "Use Your Words" as you ask AI to do most of your work for you and free up your time for the things that really matter in your life!

-Bo Yoder

P.S. I have less and less time in my life to sit down and read a physical book these days, so I'm always thankful when there are cheat sheets and downloadable resources to give me easy access to the tools taught in any books I read.

So I want you to have the same benefit...

I'm planning to create a downloadable document that includes every structure and prompt developed and optimized within the book put together in an easily accessed document.

This will allow you to easily copy and paste these complex language-based instructions into your own AI or modify and adjust them as needed to fit your unique projects.

To download the full prompt library, as well as some additional surprise bonus items, please visit:

www.AIPSprompts.com/bookbonus[1]

and let us know your best email to send those out to you!

---

1. http://www.AIPSprompts.com/bookbonus

Chapter 1
The Words That Command: Ignite AI's Infinite Potential
With the Power of Words

Language is the cornerstone of human civilization, driving progress and innovation throughout history.

From the dawn of spoken communication to the development of the written word, language has shaped our understanding of the world and enabled us to connect with one another on a deeper level.

As a species, the power of language has fueled our greatest achievements, and triggered our greatest acts of destruction, transforming us from primitive tribes to the complex societies we are today.

The evolution of language is a testament to our relentless pursuit of knowledge and our ability to adapt and innovate. As we have expanded our understanding of the world, our language has evolved to accommodate new ideas, enabling us to express complex thoughts and emotions for anybody who reads our words, even long after we are dead.

In this way, language has become the driving force behind our ability to share, learn, specialize and grow as individuals and as a species.

Throughout history, we have developed various tools to aid in the dissemination and preservation of language.

The invention of the written word marked a significant turning point in human history, as it allowed us to record our thoughts and ideas for future generations.

This breakthrough paved the way for the development of literature, science, and philosophy, transforming the way we perceive and interact with the world around us.

The invention of the printing press in the 15th century further revolutionized our ability to share knowledge. By enabling the mass production of written works, the printing press made information more accessible to the general public.

This democratization of knowledge led to an explosion of creativity and innovation, giving rise to the Renaissance and the Age of Enlightenment.

In the 20th century, the emergence of mass media, such as newspapers, radio, and television, brought about yet another transformation in our ability to communicate.

These new channels made it possible to disseminate information almost instantly, on a scale never before imagined, connecting people across vast distances and shaping the course of world events.

The advent of the internet in the late 20th century marked the beginning of a new era in human communication.

Today, the internet connects billions of people around the globe, allowing us to exchange ideas, collaborate on projects, and access a wealth of knowledge with unprecedented ease.

In many ways, the internet has become the ultimate expression of the power of language, offering us a tool with which to shape our world and make vast fortunes by connecting our products and services with people in ways we never thought possible.

As I write this, we are at the turning point of a new revolution in the use and power of language.

The introduction of large language models has transformed the AI landscape.

By leveraging the power of the language we use every day as a primary programming and instruction tool, these models have made high level AI programming and tasking more accessible to a wider audience.

No longer must you be a computer scientist who spends years mastering deeply confusing and technical programming languages in order to be able to instruct computer systems what to do!

Using "normal" language as it's primary interface and programming syntax, AI has become an invaluable resource for non-technically minded individuals and businesses alike, offering a wealth of possibilities for those who can harness its power effectively.

In this book, we will explore the importance of language as a tool for clear communication as you instruct and interact with language-based AI systems.

We will delve into the myriad ways in which mastering the art of conversational programming can empower you to unlock the full potential of AI, transforming your life and your work in ways you never thought possible.

By learning how to communicate effectively with AI, you can "tell it what to do" for you.

Harnessing its power to work for you tirelessly and efficiently, without complaint, pay, or the need for breaks or vacations.

The key lies in your ability to think and write or speak in simple, clear language and express your thoughts and instructions in a way that even the most sophisticated AI "mind" can understand and execute.

Throughout this book, I will guide you through the process of developing the skills necessary to collaborate with AI, from crafting the perfect programming "prompt" to fine-tuning your instructions via iterations and follow up questions for maximum clarity and efficiency.

Along the way, I will share examples, case studies, and practical exercises designed to help you become proficient in the art of conversational natural language programming.

As we embark on this journey together, I invite you to reflect on the power of language as a driving force behind human progress.

Just as our ancestors used the written word to shape the course of history, so too can we use the power of carefully crafted language to shape the future of AI and radically grow our businesses.

As we begin our exploration of the power of language in AI, let us first change our thinking about these AI agents who we will be asking to work on our behalf.

Rather than thinking of them as computers, machines, or robots, it will be far simpler to consider them using the concept of an employee avatar—a virtual assistant, butler, or minion who is hardworking and well-intentioned but lacks the ability to think creatively for themselves.

This employee avatar relies on your clear, logical, and well-structured instructions to carry out their tasks and produce the desired results.

In many ways, this simplistic human avatar concept serves as a metaphor for AI, highlighting the importance of effective communication in unlocking its full potential.

As you will see moving forward, the product of your AI's work is only as good as the instructions, outlines, structures and details about the desired outcome that went into the original request.

As programmers have been saying for decades...

"Garbage in, Garbage out".

In the chapters to come, we will delve deeper into the intricacies of conversational natural language programming, providing you with the tools and techniques you need to become proficient in this now essential skill.

I hope that this journey will inspire you to embrace the power of language as a tool for change and growth, not just in the realm of AI, but in all aspects of your life.

As we stand on the brink of a new era in human history, we are witnessing the arrival of a new paradigm, as this groundbreaking technology promises to revolutionize the way we communicate, work, and live.

With its unparalleled potential to process vast amounts of data, learn from experience, and adapt to new situations, AI has the power to transform every aspect of our lives, from the way we conduct and grow our businesses to the way we interact with one another.

One of the most exciting aspects of AI is its potential to revolutionize communication and eliminate many of the pitfalls that have long plagued human interactions.

By harnessing the power of AI, we can overcome the limitations of our own understanding and break down the barriers that often stand in the way of clear, effective communication.

One of the most remarkable characteristics of AI is its ability to work tirelessly and continuously improve itself over time.

Unlike human workers, who require rest, compensation, and other forms of support, AI can operate on demand, without plans or schedules around the clock.

This makes AI an invaluable asset for businesses and individuals alike, enabling them to accomplish tasks more quickly, efficiently, and accurately than ever before.

By learning how to communicate clearly and effectively with AI, you can unleash its boundless and tireless capabilities, transforming your work, your business and your life in ways you never thought possible.

By delegating routine or repetitive tasks to AI, we can free up more time and energy to focus on higher-level activities that require creativity, empathy, contextual understanding and human judgment.

I can clearly see that in the near future, (Perhaps as you read these words it has already happened) that the "haves" will be the ones who can leverage themselves and their work using AI, while those who fail to master the skill of natural language programming will be stuck in a class of "have nots", working low wage jobs based on AI generated tasks, and instructions.

It's critical that you don't let this fundamental transformation of how work is done pass you by.

While the potential benefits of AI are immense and will continue to grow and accelerate at an astonishing rate, they can only be fully realized if we are able to communicate effectively with these "intelligent" machines, and get them to push the envelope of their limitations.

This is where the art of conversational programming comes in.

Conversational, natural language programming is the process of crafting clear, concise, and well-structured instructions that AI systems can understand and execute.

By mastering this skill, we can ensure that our interactions with AI are as productive and efficient as possible, allowing us to harness its full potential and reap the benefits it has to offer.

Clear and logical communication is absolutely essential when it comes to instructing AI.

Unlike humans, who can often infer meaning from vague or ambiguous statements, AI systems require precise, unambiguous instructions to carry out their tasks effectively.

For this reason, it is crucial that we learn to think in simple, clear language and express our thoughts and instructions in a way that even the most sophisticated AI can understand and act upon.

This may involve breaking complex tasks down into smaller, more manageable steps, or providing detailed explanations of the desired outcome.

Again, the avatar concept of a human employee, servant or minion will be very useful to you.

Imagine you ask your human employee to "Make me a sandwich".

It's likely that person would come back with something edible between two slices of bread, but there would be a great deal of randomness in the result.

It could be a soggy PB&J and still be exactly what you asked for...Which was "a sandwich".

Again, assuming we are interacting with a human we are paying to help us in our lives...

How would you communicate to your human employee, so that they know what your preferences are?

After you hired them, you might have sat down and told them all sorts of details about what you like and don't like.

How you like your coffee, and that you can't stand jelly with peanut butter and prefer honey instead.

This training or "priming" phrase is exactly the process you will go through as you get more sophisticated in your prompt engineering.

(A "prompt" is the word used to describe a series of sentences and instructions, a "text block" you give to the AI to tell it what you want it to do for you.)

The difference between a human employee and an AI is that currently, with the available technology, every prompt is given to your AI "employee" is as if it's happening on their "first day".

The way the technology works now, there isn't a memory of training phases from the past that gets retained so that you don't have to repeat yourself and your requests.

This will likely change soon, and that will reduce the number of redundant instructions needed to set and keep an AI on track in its workflow.

However, in my experience, even with big memory banks, computers get corrupted regularly through normal use and need to be "rebooted", so I suspect that the "training language" aspect of prompt engineering will not go away any time soon.

So, with this understanding...

"Make me a sandwich."

Becomes...

"Please make me a sandwich on toasted sourdough bread. I'd like it to have ¼ lb smoked turkey and two slices of the Swiss cheese that's in the second drawer of the fridge. Please put a tiny amount of mustard and a generous amount of mayonnaise, and add some fresh ground pepper on top of the mayo. I'd like spring greens instead of iceberg lettuce and only two slices of tomato so it doesn't drip all over. Put it on a big plate and bring it to me here with two napkins so I can keep writing. After you have made the sandwich, please put all it's nutritional information into my food log so I can keep track of my macro and micro nutrients for the day. Thank you."

Close your eyes for a moment and visualize this interaction with a real human in the real world.

With this level of explicit clarity, how can you expect to get anything except exactly the sandwich you want?

This is your first taste of how an effective prompt is truly "engineered".

By honing our ability to communicate clearly and effectively with AI, we can ensure that our interactions with these powerful machines are as accurate and productive as possible.

In the coming chapters, we will delve deeper into the art of conversational natural language programming, providing you with the tools, techniques, and insights you need to become proficient in this essential skill.

Through examples, case studies, and practical exercises, you will learn how to craft the perfect prompt, fine-tune your instructions for maximum clarity and efficiency, and unlock the full potential of AI.

I want this book to stand the test of time, which is a challenge, given the pace of innovation and change in the AI space.

I plan to try and keep the instructions and examples as universal as possible, so that no matter how AI evolves and changes over the years, your ability to converse with it and craft the best possible prompts for the best possible responses using your natural language skills will be unchanged.

We will dig into a wide array of potential applications for AI, from customer support and content creation to sales and lead generation, market research, product development and beyond.

With each chapter, you will gain a deeper understanding of the potential of AI and the crucial role that clear communication plays in unlocking its full power.

Through real-world examples and actual work flows, you will develop the skills and confidence needed to navigate the rapidly evolving landscape of AI technology and seize the opportunities it presents.

As we explore the many facets of AI and the art of conversational programming, it is important to remember that this technology is still in its infancy. While AI has made remarkable strides in recent years, there is still much we have yet to learn and discover about its capabilities and potential applications.

Yet, the future is undeniably bright, and the opportunities for growth, learning, and innovation are virtually limitless. By embracing the power of language and harnessing the potential of AI, we stand at the threshold of a new era of human achievement and progress.

Together, let us harness the power of words to command the infinite potential of AI, and embark on a journey of discovery, growth, and transformation that will change the way we live, work, and communicate forever.

Throughout history, the power of words has shaped the world in profound and lasting ways, for better or worse.

Great speeches have galvanized nations, inspired revolutions, and given voice to the hopes and dreams of millions.

At the same time, words have been wielded as weapons to manipulate, deceive, and perpetuate suffering and division.

One striking example of the power of words to inspire change is Martin Luther King Jr.'s iconic "I Have a Dream" speech.

Delivered during the 1963 March on Washington, King's impassioned call for racial equality and an end to discrimination resonated deeply with millions of Americans and helped to galvanize the civil rights movement.

In contrast, Adolf Hitler's fiery oratory played a significant role in his rise to power and the ensuing horrors of the Holocaust.

His ability to captivate and manipulate his audience through the power of words paved the way for one of the darkest chapters in human history.

These examples serve as a stark reminder of the responsibility that comes with wielding the power of language.

As we enter a new era of AI-driven communication, it is more important than ever to use language with care and intention, particularly when interacting with AI, because while humans are trying to insert filters and limits into AI, at it's core it is simply a mechanical thing and can't always be trusted.

Just as industrial accidents happen, so will AI "go off the rails" and cause damage.

As AI becomes increasingly integrated into our lives, we must be mindful of the potential for misunderstandings and miscommunications.

While AI is capable of processing and interpreting human language with remarkable accuracy, it is not infallible. It is our responsibility to ensure that our communications with AI are clear, concise, and unambiguous.

One of the challenges in working with AI is the potential for struggle with humor and other misunderstandings.

While AI has made significant strides in understanding and generating natural language, it can still struggle with the nuances of humor, sarcasm, and idiomatic expressions. This can lead to misinterpretations, unexpected output, or even humorous "hallucinations."

Take, for example, the following conversation between a user and an AI assistant:

User: "Can you tell me a silly joke about a bicycle?"

AI: "Why did the bicycle go to bed early?

Because it was two-tired!"

While the AI has generated a pun-based joke as requested, it may not be apparent to the AI that this particular joke might not be funny to all humans.

The AI is limited by its training data and may not fully understand the complexity of human humor. It cannot "know it's audience" the way we can with all our social skills and experiences interacting with others that we have had in our lives.

These AI-generated misunderstandings highlight the importance of verifying and editing AI output, particularly when using AI for professional or public-facing communications.

It is essential to review AI-generated content for clarity, accuracy, factuality and appropriateness, and to make any necessary edits or revisions to ensure that the final output meets the desired standards.

Ultimately, the key to avoiding humorous but potentially problematic situations with AI lies in treating it much like any other collaborator: providing clear instructions, maintaining open communication, and setting expectations for quality and accuracy.

By doing so, you can harness the power of AI to enhance your work, streamline your processes, and elevate your communication to new heights—all while sidestepping the pitfalls and pratfalls that can sometimes accompany AI-generated content.

As we move forward in our journey of harnessing the power of AI, it is crucial to remember that while AI is an incredibly powerful tool, it is still just that—a tool.

Humans love to anthropomorphize pets and things, and this natural tendency should be avoided when it comes to AI.

It is our responsibility to guide and shape the use of AI in a way that reflects our values, goals, and vision for the future.

When used thoughtfully and responsibly, AI has the potential to revolutionize the way we communicate, collaborate, and create.

By keeping in mind the lessons of history and the power of words, we can ensure that AI is a force for good, helping us to accelerate our building of the future world.

As we conclude this chapter, we invite you to take an active role in the AI revolution!

Embrace the power of words, learn to effectively harness the potential of AI, and embark on a journey of unbounded growth and learning.

Now that philosophy stuff is out of the way, the rest of this book will delve deeper into specific techniques and applications, equipping you with the knowledge and skills necessary to navigate the emerging world of AI.

Together, we'll explore the art of prompt crafting, learn how to assemble the perfect AI dream team, and master various applications of AI, from customer support to market research, product development, and beyond.

I'll share case studies, anecdotes, and practical advice to help you hone your skills and make the most of AI's boundless capabilities.

Chapter 2

Demystifying AI:

Embrace the Future by Mastering the Art of Conversational Programming

As we move into a future where AI becomes more and more integrated into our daily lives, it's essential to understand how to communicate effectively with and accurately command these powerful tools.

Many people approach AI with misconceptions and engage in practices that may not yield the desired results.

They dismiss AI as "not worth it" and give up enormous power by resisting what will ultimately be a massive societal shift in the way work is done.

One of the most common pitfalls when communicating with AI is providing vague instructions using generalized language.

AI systems rely on the information you give them to generate relevant and accurate responses.

If your instructions are unclear, the AI may struggle to understand your intent and produce suboptimal results based on false assumptions as it tries as hard as it can to fill in the blanks left in your prompt.

Simply put, if you ask an AI to "write an article," it won't know what topic you want the article to be about, the target audience, the desired tone, or the required length.

A more effective approach would be to provide specific details about the desired output, using a prompt such as this.

"Please write me a 1,000-word article for an audience who loves golf about the latest advancements in putter technology, focusing on the benefits of recent advancements in material science and training techniques. Thank you."

In this example prompt, you have explicitly constrained the focus and attention of the AI on the structure and content you wish it to generate.

1. **Length:** 1,000 words
2. **Who is this for:** Lovers of golf
3. **Topic:** Cutting edge putter breakthroughs
4. **Focus:** New materials and training techniques

Again, shifting this prompts target audience mentally from a machine mind to that of a human freelance writer can help make this language structure make sense.

If you were hiring a freelancer you had never interacted with before to write this for you, what you have to tell them in order to get the best possible outcome for your money spent?

Checklists and frameworks like this can help you improve your requests, and the beauty of AI is that you can ask it to write or suggest improvements to prompts for itself!

These "co-generated" prompts can be the most effective since you asked the "mind" that will be doing the work to help you structure the instructions in a manner that works best for it!

We will dig deeper into the topic of co-generation and co-optimization in another chapter...

It's important to note that while it's essential to provide enough detailed information for the AI to understand your intent, it's equally important not to overload the system with overly complex prompts.

If you provide a prompt that is excessively long or one with multiple concepts and requests, the AI may struggle to parse the information and will likely jump to wrong conclusions and "drift" as it tries to accomplish that it believes to be its task at that moment.

Once again, think about a human avatar. If you bark out a bunch of unconnected and unrelated orders to your employee all at once, what are the odds that they will forget one or even worse misunderstand the request and do a bunch of work to produce the wrong thing?

Instead, think about all the steps needed to accomplish the task, and break down your request into smaller, more focused prompts.

You can then run a series of prompts and later combine the individual outputs to create a complete report or high-quality piece of content.

The simple advice is to make sure that you understand how important it is that each prompt addresses a single, specific goal, and avoid including extraneous information that might confuse the AI.

This will all become abundantly clear as we progress into prompt development and workflows in subsequent chapters.

AI systems are designed to process and analyze vast amounts of data. However, they still rely on the context you provide to generate meaningful and accurate responses.

Providing insufficient context is another common pitfall in AI communication and prompt engineering.

For example, if you ask an AI to "summarize the key points of the last meeting," it won't have any information about what meeting you're referring to, who attended, or what was discussed.

In this case, the AI would be unlikely to generate any response that would make sense or be useful.

To avoid this pitfall, ensure that you provide enough context for the AI to understand your request. Include relevant details, such as the meeting date, participants, and topics discussed.

The more context you provide about what matters and what does not, the better equipped the AI will be to generate a meaningful and accurate response.

Again, the human avatar concept is a useful thinking device.

If you had an important person from another region coming to a meeting you are running, wouldn't it make sense to have breakfast with that person and give them context and "color" about the purpose and agenda of the meeting and what your expectations are for their contribution?

In the following sections, we will delve deeper into the art of conversational programming and explore strategies for crafting effective prompts. By mastering these techniques, you'll be well on your way to unlocking the full potential of AI, transforming the way you work and live.

The 5 Steps For Crafting Effective Prompts

Now that we've addressed common misconceptions and pitfalls in AI communication, let's distill all we have talked about up to this point into a simple set of guidelines.

- **Define your goal clearly:** Before you start crafting a prompt, take a moment to clearly define your goal. What do you want the AI to accomplish? What should the output look like? Having a clear understanding of your objective will make it easier to craft a prompt that generates the desired results.

- **Be specific and concise and stick to one task at a time:** As we discussed earlier, providing specific and concise instructions is crucial for effective communication with AI. Make sure your prompt includes all the necessary details for the AI to understand your request but avoid including extraneous information that may confuse the system.

- **Use simple, clear language:** Although AI systems are designed to understand complex language, it's best to use simple, clear language when crafting your prompts. This makes it easier for the AI to parse your instructions and generate a relevant response.

- **Provide adequate context:** As we've mentioned before, context is essential for effective AI communication and usable work output. Be sure to include any relevant background information or details that will help the AI understand your request and generate an appropriate response.

- **Test and refine your prompts thorough iteration:** It's important to remember that AI communication is an iterative process. Don't be discouraged if your initial prompt doesn't yield the desired results. Instead, analyze the AI's response, identify any issues, and refine your prompt accordingly. With practice and patience, you'll become better at crafting effective prompts that produce the outcomes you're looking for.

Real World Examples: Putting Prompt Engineering into Practice

Now that we've discussed the basic strategies for crafting effective prompts, let's examine some real-world case studies that demonstrate how these techniques can be applied in various scenarios.

Case Study 1: Organizing Random Bits Of Relevant Information Into A Cohesive And Useful Article Length Content Piece.

Let us say that you have been tasked with the job of writing your own biography for an upcoming speaking engagement.

It's always awkward to blow your own horn, and you want some help making this bio attractive and interesting enough to make people who are looking at the program attend your lecture.

I'll use this example to run you through step by step how I would use Natural Language Programming to develop a series of prompts which will deliver the desired outcome.

First, I must carefully define my goal.

"Please write me a biography for an upcoming speaking engagement. This biography must make me look attractive and interesting as I must compete for attention from an audience deciding which speech to attend for that hour. Thank you."

This text block gives the AI a goal and some context about what the bio will be used for and what I want it to accomplish.

(Notice that throughout the book I use "please" and "thank you" in every prompt. Testing has shown that being polite to the AI produces a more human type response, instead of a more mechanical "search engine" type response. Go figure...what you were taught about manners goes for machine intelligence too!)

Now, I need to feed the AI all the information it needs about me to build the bio I am looking for.

"Here are some relevant facts about me that you can use when you write the bio.

My name is Bo Yoder

I have been an independent trader in the financial markets since 1997.

I have also worked as an edge development consultant and have coached and mentored thousands of people since 1999.

I am a founding partner at Market Forecasting Academy.

I am not a programmer, but have been breaking down complex investing and trading concepts in order to teach them to others, and in addition I have hired many freelancers and outsourced many tasks over the years, so building a clear and simple request for somebody else to follow to do specific work for me has been a core skill set for many decades.

I have written 2 books on trading which were published by McGraw-Hill and wrote a daily column for TheStreet.com for a number of years, so writing and using language to express myself are a core part of my career.

I am passionate about productivity and time management systems as I believe that time is our ultimate currency.

Self-discipline and the ability to follow through on a plan is what separates the successful from the failures in the trading and investing space. I have a strong background in neuroscience, behavioral economics and human psychology, and believe that managing the Default Mode Network's activity is the key to human happiness.

I developed an accelerated personal growth technique I call The Myalolipsis Technique to suppress the default mode network and open a direct channel to the subconscious for rapid drug free behavior and habit change which helps my clients break through their psychological and self-discipline issues when scaling their trading business.

The skills I use to help clients reprogram their subconscious mind to overcome self-limiting beliefs and habits are almost exactly the same skills needed to tell an AI what you want it to do for you, so this has helped me leap ahead in this field.

I am a life long autodidact. My only school experience was when I went to Boston University and received an MBA. Never did any bachelors degree.

Having entered the trading field just as the day trading revolution began, I see AI as being a societally shifting breakthrough and my unique career has given me a series of skills that are perfectly aligned to interacting and programing natural language AI models, the same way I have been prompting and programming human clients natural intelligence using my Myalolipsis technique for years."

Notice how this list is disorganized, unclear, and has some bad grammar and strange sentence structure as well.

If I feed this prompt just as it is into a LLM, let's see what the bio looks like.

Because there will likely be iterations, optimizations and tweaks needed to produce the bio I want, I will copy this "Ver 1.0" output into a text document to capture every step of the "development" cycle as I craft the language and instructions contained within the prompt."

VER 1.0 Output:

Introducing our extraordinary speaker for today's event, Bo Yoder is an accomplished individual with a vast array of skills and experiences that span over two decades. A pioneer in the financial markets since 1997, our speaker has achieved remarkable success as an independent trader and edge development consultant. Through coaching and mentoring thousands of people since 1999, they have demonstrated an innate ability to break down complex investing and trading concepts for others to understand and apply.

Our speaker has authored two highly-regarded books on trading, published by McGraw-Hill, and contributed to TheStreet.com with a daily column for several years. Their passion for writing and clear communication has played a pivotal role in their illustrious career.

With an unwavering commitment to productivity and time management, our speaker firmly believes that time is our ultimate currency. A strong advocate of self-discipline, they have delved deep into the realms of neuroscience, behavioral economics, and human psychology, asserting that managing the Default Mode Network's activity is the key to human happiness.

As a life-long autodidact, our speaker's only formal education was an MBA from Boston University. Despite this, they developed The Myalolipsis Technique, an accelerated personal growth method that suppresses the default mode network and opens a direct channel to the subconscious for rapid, drug-free behavior and habit change. This innovative technique has been instrumental in helping clients overcome self-limiting beliefs and habits.

With the advent of AI and its potential to revolutionize society, our speaker has leveraged their unique career experiences to excel in the field of natural language AI models. Their expertise in reprogramming the subconscious mind using The Myalolipsis Technique has seamlessly translated into directing AI to accomplish specific tasks.

Join us as our captivating speaker shares their wealth of knowledge and insights, guaranteed to leave you inspired and motivated. This is an opportunity you won't want to miss!

Ok, out comes this 300-word bio.

It's a start but it isn't what I want.

Again, I use the avatar concept to define the issues I want to fix in the second iteration.

If this was the work product of a human writer, how would I critique and instruct that human to make my changes?

The beauty of this advancement into natural language programming is that your instructions are pretty much the same for either a human or an AI.

Rather than starting over from scratch, I will just ask the AI to make the necessary changes and it will remember my previous interactions, so I don't have to resubmit my details again.

Iteration 1 Prompt

"This is a good start, but there are some changes I'd like you to make. Please rewrite this bio and make the following changes.

Make it about half as long.

Make it less bombastic, it has the tone of a circus ringleader. Please use a less emotional and professional tone.

My name is Bo Yoder, you said "our speaker", likely because I forgot to put my name into the original prompt, my bad.

The fact that they accepted me into an MBA program without any formal schooling or any bachelors degree is a good thing! You said I developed Myalolipsis "despite" this. Please change that bias and celebrate this fact instead. Thank you."

Can you see this block of text being sent as an email to a human writer?

Are you starting to get excited about the possibilities of using your current language skills to instruction complex computer systems to do significant work for you?

You should be!

Here is the revised version the AI spit out after taking in my list of requests for iteration.

Iteration 1 output

Introducing Bo Yoder, an accomplished independent trader and edge development consultant with a rich background in the financial markets since 1997. Bo has excelled in coaching and mentoring thousands of people, skillfully simplifying complex investing and trading concepts. Bo is also a published author, having written two books on trading and contributing a daily column to TheStreet.com for several years.

Bo's dedication to productivity and time management is reflected in his passion for neuroscience, behavioral economics, and human psychology. He developed The Myalolipsis Technique, a

groundbreaking personal growth method that enables rapid, drug-free behavior and habit change.

As a testament to Bo's exceptional self-driven learning abilities, he earned an MBA from Boston University without any prior formal schooling or a bachelor's degree. His innovative Myalolipsis Technique has not only been transformative for his clients but has also provided him with valuable skills to excel in the field of natural language AI models.

Join us for an engaging session with Bo Yoder as he shares his expertise and insights, sure to leave a lasting impact on all attendees.

The length at 177 words is a lot better, and the tone is much cleaner and more professional.

It's basically what I wanted, but there are a few tweaks I want to make to clarify things and make it exactly the way I want.

So, I just pasted this text into a word processor and made my edits and here is the final product.

Final Version (Human Edited)

Today's speaker Bo Yoder, is a two time author and accomplished independent trader since 1997 and edge development consultant with a rich background in the financial markets.

Bo has coached and mentored thousands of people, simplifying complex investing and trading concepts so that anybody can master the skill of trading.

Bo is also a published author, having written numerous magazine articles, as well as two books on trading and wrote a daily column for TheStreet.com for several years.

Bo's dedication to productivity and time management is reflected in his passion for understanding the neuroscience, behavioral economics, and human psychology that drives human behavior inside and outside the financial markets.

He is the developer of The Myalolipsis Technique, a groundbreaking personal growth method that enables rapid, drug-free behavior and habit change though non-ordinary states of consciousness where deep learning at a neural level is accelerated.

This breakthrough has not only been transformative for his trading clients, helping them to develop effortless discipline, but has also provided him with valuable skills to excel in the field of natural language programming for AI models.

A lifelong autodidact, Bo earned an MBA from Boston University without any prior formal schooling or a bachelor's degree.

Please join us at 10:00am in Ballroom 2B for an engaging session entitled ""Talk Your Way to Wealth: Harnessing Conversational AI to Unearth Hidden Financial Opportunities".

This real world example show the power to compress time and accomplish a task that used to take 30-60 minutes into literally 15 minutes or less.

It also shows the collaborative nature of natural language programming...The bottega workshop structure laid out right before your eyes.

Also, for coders or anybody who has worked on developing software, notice how when the first iteration's output wasn't what I wanted, I didn't have to wipe everything and go back to editing the original prompt?

I can just take the work that has been done before and have a new version made with my edits and suggestions incorporated.

Version after version, in different lengths, styles, tones...

Whatever I want to play with or experiment with.

All with no burden of additional cost, nobody getting offended because their work isn't being accepted, no resentment about being asked to repeat and revise over and over again.

This is the magical new world that we see emerging as we can for the first time just "talk our way to wealth".

The Iterative Prompting Process: Refining and Testing for Optimal Results

Just as with any skill, harnessing the full potential of AI through conversational natural language programming requires practice and an understanding of the inherent iterative nature of the process.

Iteration is a critical aspect of working with language based Large Language Model AI systems.

Since the AI language models are not perfect, they can sometimes generate unexpected or less-than-ideal results.

By iteratively refining your prompts and testing the AI's responses to different instructions, you can progressively improve the quality of the output until you achieve your desired outcome.

To further illustrate the importance of iterative prompting, let's consider the analogy of learning to play a musical instrument.

When someone first starts learning an instrument, they typically begin by learning the basics, such as how to hold the instrument and play simple notes.

As they progress, they practice more complex techniques and pieces, refining their skills through repetition and feedback.

In this analogy, the AI Large Language Model can be thought of as the instrument, and the prompt engineer – you – are the musician.

Like a musician learning to play an instrument, you must practice and refine your approach to crafting prompts to achieve the best possible results from the AI.

Here are some key parallels between learning to play a musical instrument and mastering the art of conversational programming with AI:

- **Start with the basics:** Just as a musician begins by learning simple notes and techniques, you should start by understanding the basic principles of effective prompting, such as being clear, concise, and specific in your instructions.

- **Practice and repetition:** Becoming proficient at an instrument requires consistent practice and repetition. Similarly, to become skilled at crafting effective prompts, you should practice regularly and experiment with different techniques and approaches.

- **Seek feedback and learn from mistakes:** A musician often seeks feedback from teachers or peers to identify areas for improvement. In the context of AI, this feedback comes from the AI's responses to your prompts. By analyzing the AI's output and identifying any shortcomings, you can refine your prompts and learn from your mistakes.

- **Adapt to the instrument's strengths and limitations:** Every musical instrument has unique strengths and limitations, and a skilled musician learns to adapt their playing style accordingly. Similarly, different AI language models have their own strengths and weaknesses, and understanding these can help you tailor your prompts or choose different AI systems for specific tasks for optimal results.

- **Experiment, play and explore:** Great musicians often push the boundaries of their instrument by experimenting with new techniques and styles. In the same vein, don't be afraid to explore the full range of possibilities with AI and experiment with different types of prompts to unlock new and creative applications. Worst case, you get an output that's not useful, so you throw it away and try again with an adjusted prompt.

By approaching AI conversational programming with the mindset of learning a musical instrument, you can gradually refine your ability to craft effective prompts through iteration and practice, ultimately harnessing the power of AI to achieve your goals.

Introducing the "5 Steps" Framework for Organizing Thoughts and Crafting Effective Prompts

The key to successful communication with AI lies in the ability to organize your thoughts and craft efficient prompts that accurately convey your goals and desired outcomes.

In this section, we will introduce a step-by-step framework to guide you through the process of organizing your thoughts and crafting effective prompts that produce the desired output.

By following this framework, you can ensure a more seamless collaboration with the various available AI systems, leading to higher-quality results and greater overall success.

Step 1: Define Your Goal with Examples For The AI To Use And Mimic

The first step in crafting an efficient prompt is to define your goal clearly, both for yourself and for the AI you wish to instruct.

This means understanding exactly what you want to achieve and how the AI can help you reach that objective.

Take the time to consider the purpose of the task, the information you need, and the results you want to obtain.

Example 1: If you are a content writer, your goal might be to create a well-researched and engaging article on a specific topic. In this case, you may want to use the AI to help you generate ideas, create an outline, or draft the content.

Example 2: If you are a sales manager, your goal could be to improve your team's lead qualification process. Here, the AI could assist by engaging prospects on your website or through email campaigns and help qualify leads based on predefined criteria.

By defining your goal, clearly and explicitly, you can establish a clear direction for the AI, ensuring that it stays focused on delivering the results you desire.

Step 2: Define the Desired Output with Examples So The AI Can Better Understand Your Expectations

Once you have defined your goal, the next step is to define the desired output. This means specifying the format and expected content of the AI's response.

Be as detailed and explicit as possible, as this will provide the AI with the necessary context to generate accurate and relevant results.

Example 1: If your goal is to create an article on a specific topic, the desired output could be a list of potential subtopics, a detailed outline, or a completed draft. Be specific about the structure, tone, and style you want the AI to incorporate into the content.

Example 2: For a sales manager looking to improve lead qualification, the desired output might be a series of qualifying questions the AI can ask prospects or a script for AI-generated emails that help determine the prospect's level of interest and fit.

Clearly defining the desired output ensures that the AI understands what you expect from its responses and can tailor its approach accordingly.

Step 3: Break Down the Task into Smaller Steps with Examples

Next, break down the task into smaller steps to simplify the process for the AI.

By dividing the task into manageable components, you can provide the AI with a clear roadmap to follow, increasing the likelihood of obtaining accurate and relevant results.

Example 1: For a content writer, breaking down the task of creating an article might involve the following steps:

1) Generate a list of potential subtopics;

2) Create a detailed outline based on the chosen subtopics; 3) Draft the content following the outline.

Example 2: A sales manager looking to improve lead qualification might break down the task into these steps:

1) Identify the key qualifying criteria;

2) Develop a set of questions or a script to gather the

necessary information from prospects;

3) Use AI-generated responses to evaluate and qualify leads

based on the gathered information.

Breaking down tasks into smaller steps helps the AI to better understand the overall process and deliver more focused and relevant results.

Step 4: Craft the Initial Prompt with Examples So That the AI Has The Context Needed

With your goal defined, desired output identified, and the task broken down into smaller steps, you can now craft the initial prompt for the AI.

Use clear, concise language and provide enough context to help the AI understand your expectations and requirements.

Remember to be specific about the format and content of the desired output to ensure the AI generates the most relevant results.

Example 1: For a content writer seeking ideas for an article on vertical hydroponics, the initial prompt might be:

"Please generate a list of 10 engaging and well-researched subtopics for an article on vertical hydroponics, aimed at a general audience without knowledge of this subject. Focus on benefits and reasons for vertical hydroponics and include actionable tips and strategies that individuals can implement to grow a kitchen herb garden in an extremely limited space. Thank you."

Example 2: For a sales manager looking to improve lead qualification, the initial prompt could be:

"Please develop a series of 5 qualifying questions that our AI can use to engage with prospects visiting our website, focusing on determining their level of interest in our product and their compatibility with our target customer profile. Thank you."

By crafting a clear and focused initial prompt, you set the stage for the AI to generate accurate and useful responses that align with your goals and desired outcomes.

Step 5: Test and Refine the Prompt with Examples

Finally, test your prompt with the AI and evaluate the results.

Remember that the process of crafting efficient prompts is often iterative, requiring adjustments and refinements based on the AI's responses.

Use the feedback from the AI's work product to identify areas for improvement and make necessary adjustments to the prompt, ensuring that it is as clear and effective as possible.

Example 1: If the content writer's initial prompt resulted in a list of subtopics that were too broad or unrelated to sustainable living, they could refine the prompt by specifying the desired focus, such as:

"Please generate a list of 10 engaging and well-researched subtopics specifically related to getting started with vertical hydroponics using just 1 square foot of space on your balcony or deck. Thank you."

Example 2: If the sales manager's initial prompt produced qualifying questions that were too generic or did not address the specific needs of their target customers, they could refine the prompt by adding more context:

"Please develop a series of 5 qualifying questions for our AI to engage with prospects visiting our website, focusing on their level of interest in our software solution for small to medium-sized businesses and their current challenges with project management. Thank you."

By testing and refining the prompt through multiple iterations, you can ensure that the AI generates the most accurate and relevant results, ultimately leading to a more successful collaboration with the Large Language Model AI systems you are working with.

Let's go through a real-world example step by step as we use the framework above to create a complex prompt, with multiple steps and an iterative process built in for optimized output.

The Bottega Model: Collaborating With AI To Write The Best Performing Prompts Possible.

My goal for this next prompt is to build an "AIPS" (Artificial Intelligence Personality Simulation) to help you build, refine and simplify your own prompts.

As a human being, you have spent your life interacting with humans. In my opinion, one of the most powerful things about natural language programming is that it lets you use

your existing skill set of communication and social skills in order to interact with the machine world.

Therefore, the AIPS concept is a core one for me as I find that I am most effective, efficient and productive when I work on complex projects with an AIPS personality simulation vs thinking of the AI as just a machine.

So, the first thing I want to define in this prompt development process is exactly who I will be interacting with.

"Please play the role of a specialist in effective natural language prompt development, with a vast knowledge of best practices and tips and tricks to create the best prompts possible."

Now that I have told the AI what role I want it to simulate, it's area of focus and expertise and how we will address each other throughout this interaction, I can move to the next step.

In this next block of this prompt, I will tell the AI the steps I want it to go through in clear and explicit language.

"The goal for this session is to build a prompt that will be structured in the best and clearest way for you to use and understand. I will paste in a detailed framework for all the steps we need to go through together. Once you understand the framework, please interview me in a conversational style to walk me through all the steps of this framework as we work together to build the best possible prompt. At the appropriate points where a decision needs to be made, please ask me questions and use my answers to guide your actions as we work through the framework together. Thank you. Here is the framework I want you to use."

If I now paste in the code blocks listed above, and then the entire 1,092 word text of the "Introducing the Step-by-Step Framework for Organizing Thoughts and Crafting Effective Prompts" framework I laid out above into the AI, I get the following interaction...

Thank you for providing the Step-by-Step Framework for Organizing Thoughts and Crafting Effective Prompts. I'm excited to help you build the best possible prompt using this framework. Let's start by working through each step together. Please feel free

to provide any additional information you think might be relevant during our conversation.

Step 1: Define Your Goal with Examples For The AI To Use And Mimic

Could you please tell me the goal you want to achieve with the AI's assistance?

I replied...

"My goal is to create a highly simplified and optimized prompt for a prompt engineer collaboration based on the framework I shared with you. The perfect outcome would be an optimized prompt that I can save and just paste in anytime I need help developing a new prompt in collaboration with you."

The AIPS moves on to the next step in the framework...

Step 2: Identify the Desired Output with Examples So The AI Can Better Understand Your Expectations

I understand your goal is to have a simplified and optimized prompt for a prompt engineer collaboration. For this desired output, would you like the AI to provide a template with placeholders that you can fill in according to your specific needs each time you want to create a new prompt? Or do you have a different format in mind for the output? Please provide an example if possible.

I replied...

"Please use the framework I shared with you earlier and lead me through the process. My goal is to be able to develop a prompt that gives you enough information to lead anybody, no matter their skill

set or level of expertise through this framework so that they can create sophisticated and effective prompts for their own needs."

The AIPS replies...

Thank you for the clarification. Let's proceed with the framework and develop the prompt together.

Step 3: Break Down the Task into Smaller Steps with Examples

Based on your goal, I suggest breaking down the task into the following smaller steps:

1. Understand the user's goal for their prompt.
2. Identify the desired output format and any specific examples.
3. Guide the user through the process of creating a prompt by asking relevant questions and providing suggestions.
4. Help the user refine their prompt through testing and iterations.

Step 4: Craft the Initial Prompt with Examples So That the AI Has The Context Needed

With the smaller steps identified, let's craft an initial prompt for the AI:

"Help me create a new prompt using the Step-by-Step Framework for Organizing Thoughts and Crafting Effective Prompts. Begin by asking me questions to understand my goal, and then proceed to guide me through the process of creating and refining my prompt to ensure its effectiveness."

Step 5: Test and Refine the Prompt with Examples

Now, let's test the initial prompt:

Please provide any feedback on this initial prompt or let me know if you'd like to make any changes or refinements.

This is looking pretty good on the surface, but I detect a fatal flaw in this first iteration.

At this point, the AIPS has all the information and context contained in the 1,000 words I pasted in describing the framework.

If I paste in the proposed prompt into a new session, the AIPS won't have any of this context and for that matter will not know what framework I'm talking about.

I need to instruct the AIPS to add this context as it understands it, in its own language to the prompt. In addition, I think it would be good if the AIPS offers suggestions for improvement and offers a quality "grade" as part of this process.

So, now I will go into the next iteration with this guidance language.

"I want this prompt to work well in a new session, so can you please rewrite it to include whatever information is relevant so that you or another LLM has the context and the structure of the framework needed to produce a consistent and excellent outcome? In addition, I would like for you to offer suggestions for improvement of the prompt from your unique perspective, and grade the current iteration on a 1-100 scale. Please include instructions for this grading and suggestion process into the prompt on it's next iteration. Thank you."

The AIPS replies...

I have revised the initial prompt to include the necessary context and added instructions for grading and offering suggestions. Here's the updated version:

" Collaborate with me to create an effective prompt using the following framework: defining the goal, identifying the desired output, breaking down the task into smaller steps, crafting the initial prompt, and testing and refining the prompt. Engage in a conversation to clarify the topic and subject, and develop a prompt that can be used in a new session with all the relevant instructions needed for consistently excellent results. After completing the process, I want you to rate the prompt's effectiveness on a 1-100 scale and offer suggestions for improvement, while asking relevant questions to clarify my needs and incorporating them into the revised prompt."

Please let me know if you have any feedback or would like to make any additional changes to the revised prompt.

This looks like a good first attempt. I will test it by opening new session and running this prompt to see what happens.

When fed this co-generated prompt in a new session, the AIPS responds with...

Great! I'd be happy to help you create an effective prompt. To get started, let's clarify the topic and subject you'd like to focus on. Can you please provide some more information about the goal you want to achieve with the prompt?

Let's test this new AIPS by having it help me develop a prompt to write a unique bedtime story for my son.

"My goal is to create a prompt I can run every night to write a unique and entertaining bedtime story for a three year old boy named Max. I want the bedtime story to take about 15 minutes to read, and I want it to be different every day so that the stories don't repeat. I want the prompt to ask me about Max's day, so that the story can incorporate

the highlights of his day as well as any accomplishments he may have had and to reinforce any hard lessons he had to learn."

The AIPS responds...

Thank you for providing the context. Let's work on creating the prompt using the given framework:

Defining the goal:

The goal is to create a prompt that generates a unique and entertaining 15-minute bedtime story for a three-year-old boy named Max, incorporating the highlights, accomplishments, and any hard lessons from his day.

Identifying the desired output:

The output should be a well-structured, engaging bedtime story that is different every day and tailored to Max's daily experiences.

Breaking down the task into smaller steps:

a. Gather information about Max's day (highlights, accomplishments, hard lessons)

b. Create a storyline that includes the gathered information

c. Develop a captivating narrative with age-appropriate language and themes

d. Ensure the story's length is suitable for a 15-minute reading session

Crafting the initial prompt:

"Please generate a unique and entertaining bedtime story for a three-year-old boy named Max that takes about 15 minutes to read.

Max's day included the following highlights: [insert highlights], accomplishments: [insert accomplishments], and hard lessons: [insert hard lessons]. Incorporate these elements into the story and make sure the narrative is engaging and age-appropriate."

Testing and refining the prompt:

At this stage, you can test the prompt by running it with different inputs for Max's day and refining it based on the results.

Now, let me rate the effectiveness of the prompt on a 1-100 scale and provide suggestions for improvement.

Effectiveness: 85

Suggestions for improvement:

Provide more specific guidelines for the story's structure or theme, if needed.

Add any preferences regarding the story's characters, setting, or tone.

Feel free to share your thoughts on the prompt, and let me know if you have any questions or additional requirements.

Now, I can run this prompt and just add in the details of Max's day in the area with the brackets, but I want the AI to do that work for me, so Ill ask it to incorporate some questions about these details before writing the story.

"This is a great prompt, but can you please add a step where you ask me four questions for input about Max's day, his accomplishments, and lessons learned, and any theme or scenario I want the story to be about so that you or another LLM AI can gather the necessary information for customization?"

The AIPS responds...

Certainly! I've added a step to ask you four questions about Max's day, accomplishments, lessons learned, and your desired theme or scenario. Here's the revised prompt:

Defining the goal: The goal is to create a prompt that generates a unique and entertaining 15-minute bedtime story for a three-year-old boy named Max, incorporating the highlights, accomplishments, and any hard lessons from his day.

Identifying the desired output: The output should be a well-structured, engaging bedtime story that is different every day and tailored to Max's daily experiences.

Breaking down the task into smaller steps: a. Gather information about Max's day, accomplishments, hard lessons, and desired theme or scenario by asking four questions. b. Create a storyline that includes the gathered information. c. Develop a captivating narrative with age-appropriate language and themes. d. Ensure the story's length is suitable for a 15-minute reading session.

Crafting the initial prompt: "Before generating a unique and entertaining bedtime story for a three-year-old boy named Max, please answer the following questions to provide necessary information for customization:

1. What were the highlights of Max's day today?
2. What accomplishments did Max achieve today?
3. What hard lessons did Max learn today?
4. What theme or scenario would you like the story to be about?

Once you have provided this information, I will create a bedtime story that takes about 15 minutes to read, incorporates the details you've shared, and ensures an engaging and age-appropriate narrative."

Testing and refining the prompt: At this stage, you can test the prompt by running it with different inputs for Max's day and refining it based on the results.

Now, let me rate the effectiveness of the revised prompt on a 1-100 scale and provide suggestions for improvement.

Effectiveness: 95

Suggestions for improvement:

Consider adding more questions or adjusting the current ones to further refine the story, depending on your needs.

If you have any preferences for the story's characters, setting, or tone, you can include them in the questions or the prompt.

Feel free to share your thoughts on the revised prompt, and let me know if you have any questions or additional requirements.

This looks pretty good, and notice how this prompt is written in a way where the AI is forced to lay out it's thought processes so that you can nitpick and troubleshoot if the output isn't what you are looking for!

This looks great and with a quality rating of 95 the AI seems to think this new prompt is ready for usage, but the only way to know for sure is to test it...

I will open a new chat session and paste in the prompt we have generated.

The AI responds to the co-generated prompt in a fresh session like this...

Please provide the necessary information to customize the bedtime story for Max. The questions are as follows:

1. **What were the highlights of Max's day today?**
2. **What accomplishments did Max achieve today?**
3. **What hard lessons did Max learn today?**
4. **What theme or scenario would you like the story to be about?**

Once you provide this information, I will create a bedtime story that takes about 15 minutes to read, incorporates the details you've shared, and ensures an engaging and age-appropriate narrative.

Now I just need to answer the questions, and will add a number before each answer to ensure that the AIPS can keep track so the answers are connected to the proper questions.

"1 Max had a great morning playing with his friends, and then went for a swim in the pool after his nap. 2 Max shared his pool toys very nicely with his sister. 3 He didn't eat breakfast and had to deal with hunger later that morning as a result. 4 A pool party with all the characters from the Winnie the Pooh books by A A Milne."

Now that the AIPS has all the parameters it needs, it goes to work!

Title: Max's Splendid Pooh Bear Pool Party

Once upon a time, in a warm and sunny corner of the Hundred Acre Wood, there was a little boy named Max. Max had spent a lovely morning playing with his friends and swimming in the pool. He had learned that sharing his pool toys with his sister made them both happy, but he also realized that skipping breakfast was not a good idea.

One day, as the sun shone bright and warm, Max decided to throw a pool party for all his friends from the Hundred Acre Wood. He sent out invitations to Winnie the Pooh, Piglet, Tigger, Eeyore, Rabbit, Kanga, Roo, and even little Lumpy the Heffalump. Everyone was excited to attend Max's pool party!

On the morning of the party, Max made sure to eat a big, healthy breakfast. He didn't want to be hungry while playing in the pool like last time. After breakfast, he helped his mom set up the pool area with colorful decorations, balloons, and plenty of toys for everyone to enjoy.

One by one, the guests began to arrive. Pooh Bear, wearing a big straw sun hat, brought a pot of his favorite "hunny" to share with everyone. Piglet, wearing a tiny pair of swim trunks, brought a beautiful beach ball. Tigger bounced in excitedly, wearing his striped life vest, and Eeyore, with a bright blue towel draped over his back, carried a big sun umbrella to provide shade.

Rabbit, Kanga, and Roo arrived together. Rabbit was wearing his green swim goggles, while Kanga carried Roo in her pouch, who was wearing the cutest little swim cap. Lastly, Lumpy the Heffalump arrived, shyly holding a big bag of delicious fruit for everyone to share.

Max welcomed everyone to the pool party and showed them where they could put their things. Soon, the pool was filled with laughter, splashing, and fun. Max and his sister took turns sharing their pool toys with their new friends. Everyone had a fantastic time!

Max noticed that Pooh Bear was sitting on the edge of the pool, dipping his paw into his pot of "hunny." He invited Pooh to join them in the water. "Oh, bother," Pooh said, "I can't swim very well, Max." Max, being the kind and helpful boy he was, offered to teach Pooh Bear how to swim. Pooh agreed, and Max gently guided him into the water, showing him how to kick his legs and move his arms.

As Max and Pooh practiced swimming, Tigger and Roo were having a blast splashing each other with water. Eeyore found a nice spot in the shade under his umbrella, while Piglet and Lumpy played with the beach ball. Kanga and Rabbit were busy preparing a lovely picnic for everyone to enjoy after their swim.

Once Max and Pooh had finished their swimming lesson, Max's mom announced that it was time for lunch. Everyone gathered around the picnic area, drying off and enjoying the delicious sandwiches, fruit, and of course, Pooh's "hunny." Max had learned his lesson about skipping meals, and he made sure to eat a big, delicious lunch to keep his energy up.

After lunch, Max's mom brought out a special surprise: a giant, inflatable water slide! Max and his friends took turns sliding down the slide and splashing into the pool, laughing and cheering each other on. The sun began to set, and the Hundred Acre Wood glowed with warm, golden light.

Tired but happy, Max and his friends said their goodbyes, thanking Max for the wonderful pool party. As they left, Max felt

At this point, the AI "ran out of space" and halted production mid-sentence.

I am sure this is an issue that will soon be resolved as the models get better and better. But for now, I simply tell the AI to keep working on its task without losing its place...

"Please continue from exactly where you stopped"

The AIPS picks right up where it left off...

grateful for the amazing day he had shared with his friends from the Hundred Acre Wood. Max's mom helped him clean up the pool area, and they talked about all the fun they'd had.

As the stars began to twinkle in the sky, Max put on his pajamas, brushed his teeth, and climbed into bed. As his dad tucked him in and kissed him goodnight. Max smiled, thinking about the laughter, the swimming lessons, and the joy of sharing his pool toys with his sister and his new friends.

He had learned important lessons that day: the value of sharing, the importance of eating a good meal, and that helping others can be incredibly rewarding. Max closed his eyes and drifted off to sleep, dreaming of more fun adventures in the Hundred Acre Wood with Winnie the Pooh and all his friends.

The end.

That's a pretty good story, and I would say the prompt performed as I would like it to.

Having gone through this development process, I now have created an AIPS finalized and optimized prompt "application", and I can save this text block and paste it back in to a new session any time I want the AI to generate a new story.

Unlike a standard computer application, I can adjust and modify the prompt as I wish for additional customization.

Let's run the prompt one more time, and this time when it asks about Max's day, I'll ask it to produce the story as a series of rhymes.

I open up a new session, paste in the prompt exactly as before, only this time I answer the initial set of questions this way...

The AIPS dutifully follows my instructions and produces the following story in poem form.

Title: Max's Marvelous Pooh Bear Pool Party

In a warm and sunny Hundred Acre Wood,

A little boy named Max, so happy, so good,

Played with his friends, and swam in the pool,

Sharing nicely with his sister, he knew the golden rule.

Skipping breakfast, he learned was a big mistake,

The hunger pangs later were more than he could take,

What should he do today, a pool party was planned,

With Winnie the Pooh and friends, oh, it would be so grand!

Invitations he sent to Pooh, Tigger, and Piglet,

Eeyore, Kanga, Roo, and Rabbit - all of them, you bet,

Even Lumpy the Heffalump, shy but so sweet,

To Max's amazing pool party, they all did fleet.

The morning of the party, Max ate a great feast,

No hunger would bother him, not in the least,

Decorations and toys, all set for his friends,

A fun-filled day of laughter, the joy never ends.

One by one, they arrived with their things,

Hats, towels, and goggles, the fun it all brings,

Pooh with his "hunny," Piglet with a ball,

Tigger and Eeyore, excited for it all.

Max welcomed his guests with a smile so wide,

He led them to the pool, to the waters they'd glide,

Sharing toys with his sister, a joy to behold,

Max's heart, full of kindness, was truly pure gold.

The pool was alive with laughter and splashing,

The sun shining brightly, the water reflecting and dashing,

Max noticed Pooh, sitting poolside, a paw in his pot,

A swimmer he wasn't, but Max had a thought.

"Pooh, come join us," Max said with a grin,

"I'll teach you to swim, it's a skill you can win!"

So Pooh and Max entered the pool, side by side,

Max showed Pooh the strokes, no fear to hide.

Tigger and Roo, splashing water with glee,

Eeyore in the shade, Piglet and Lumpy carefree,

Kanga and Rabbit, a picnic prepared,

The friends of the Wood, their happiness shared.

Max's mom called them over, "Lunchtime is here!"

They ate and they chatted, all feeling so dear,

Sandwiches, fruit, and of course Pooh's "hunny,"

Max had learned his lesson, his tummy felt sunny.

A surprise from Max's mom, an inflatable slide,

Down into the pool, they'd laugh as they'd glide,

Golden light from the setting sun, they played without cease,

Max's Pooh Bear pool party, a day full of peace.

Tired but happy, they said their goodbyes,

Max hugged his friends, as stars filled the skies,

Cleaning up with his mom, he thought of his day,

Helping others, sharing, and fun all the way.

Tucked into bed, Max dreamed of the Wood,

Adventures with Pooh, Piglet, and the rest, oh, it would be good,

Lessons he'd learned, from breakfast to sharing,

Max's marvelous pool party, a memory worth bearing.

The end.

Once a prompt is finalized and optimized, there may be one more enhancement you might wish to add.

If you have a prompt that will be used in many different ways, it can be useful to insert an easily adjusted variable statement into the text block.

In the above example, I used the Collaborative and Iterative Prompt Developer Prompt to create a customized children's story prompt for my son Max.

If I wanted to re-task that prompt to create a story for a friend's child, I could simply change the gender and name within the prompt's text block from "Max" to "Elsie", and the gender and age from "three year old" and "boy" to "7 year old" and "girl".

While this manual approach will work, it can be time consuming and in a complicated prompt with many references, it can be easy to miss one statement that needed to be changed.

Instead, you can put a variable statement in brackets in the place of the word or concept that you want to swap out.

If formatted this way, the AI will replace the bracketed word or concept with the definition you put below the main text block.

This simply means that if you have a prompt, let's say to write a personalized thank you note to somebody, you could write it like this...

"Please write a warm and friendly thank you note to [NAME] thanking them for their gift of [GIFT]

NAME = Mary

GIFT = Gift certificate to my favorite restaurant"

The brackets tell the AI that it should match up the definition you provided below in every instance where the defined variable is used within the text block.

This allows you to use this same prompt over and over to write thank you notes to different people, thanking them for different things.

If we run this prompt as written above, the AI comes back with the following thank you note.

Dear Mary,

I hope this note finds you well and in good spirits. I wanted to take a moment to express my heartfelt gratitude for the thoughtful gift you sent my way. Receiving a gift certificate to my favorite restaurant was an absolutely delightful surprise!

Your generosity and kindness truly made my day, and I can't wait to indulge in a delicious meal at the restaurant. It's always a pleasure to share good food and create lasting memories, and your gift will certainly contribute to that.

Thank you once again, Mary, for your thoughtful gesture. I feel so fortunate to have you in my life, and I look forward to catching up with you soon. Perhaps we can even enjoy a meal together at the restaurant!

Wishing you all the best and sending warm regards,

[Your Name]

I hope these fun little exercises have entertained and inspired you, as I introduce you to the endless and quite fluid possibilities these Large Language Models provide!

You can see now how once a sophisticated prompt has been developed, it can be modified quickly and easily to meet your changing needs.

With just an additional sentence of instruction, I could run the bedtime story prompt and have this story written in Spanish, take place on the moon, incorporate any fantasy characters or Max's actual friends into the adventure.

The possibilities are literally only limited by your imagination and the willingness to ask the AI for something new!

So, in conclusion, crafting efficient prompts that accurately convey your goals and desired outcomes is crucial for successful communication with AI systems.

By using the prompt development collaborator AIPS prompt we built here together, the AI will take charge of the process and help guide you as you follow the step-by-step framework.

This will help you to organize your thoughts, define your goals, and craft effective prompts that lead to higher-quality results and amazing success when working with AI.

Embrace this process and this collaborative AIPS prompt to harness the power of AI to achieve your objectives and unlock new opportunities for growth and learning.

Chapter 3
Crafting Your AI Dream Team: Assembling the Perfect Group Of AIPS Assistants for Unstoppable Success

———

Once you begin to understand the power of using roles, avatars and other aspects of the AIPS (Artificial intelligence personality simulator) concept, it will be simple and intuitive for you to realize how to take a flat, kind of boring machine "intelligence" and transform into "Your silicon pal who's fun to be with"...Everything changes.

By getting a bit childish and "playing" with the possibilities of AI, you will open your imagination to new possibilities you had never considered before.

Again, I want to reinforce that by creating an "imaginary friend" front end on your prompts, you are harnessing all the thousands of hours you have spent interacting with other humans throughout your life for a much higher quality interaction as you will see in the examples we will go through in this book.

The best thing about these language based systems is that you don't have to learn a new programming language, syntax, rhythm, or structure.

You can just talk to your AI and have it do most of your work for you!

As an example, lets take two similar prompts and compare the user experience as well as the AI's outputs...

PROMPT 1: Stilted "Computerese"

"Give me a list of the bestselling books of all time on [Topic], with sales numbers and date of release.

Topic = sales"

That request is the sort of thing that you might send into a search engine. It's inhuman, factual and without the color, context, or nuance that language can give to a request for information or help between two people.

When fed that simple prompt, the AI returned this list of information.

1. **How to Win Friends and Influence People by Dale Carnegie - Over 30 million copies sold - 1936**
2. **The Psychology of Selling by Brian Tracy - Over 1 million copies sold - 1985**
3. **Influence: The Psychology of Persuasion by Robert Cialdini - Over 5 million copies sold - 1984**
4. **SPIN Selling by Neil Rackham - Over 1 million copies sold - 1988**
5. **The Challenger Sale by Brent Adamson and Matthew Dixon - Over 500,000 copies sold - 2011**
6. **Little Red Book of Selling by Jeffrey Gitomer - Over 1.5 million copies sold - 2004**
7. **Selling to Big Companies by Jill Konrath - Over 200,000 copies sold - 2005**
8. **The Sales Bible by Jeffrey Gitomer - Over 1 million copies sold - 1994**
9. **The Art of Closing the Sale by Brian Tracy - Over 1 million copies sold - 1984**
10. **To Sell Is Human by Daniel H. Pink - Over 1 million copies sold - 2012**

From that simple "query" prompt, the AI produces an accurate data filled list as expected.

So, it didn't fail in its task, but the prompt didn't allow any room to produce a really useful and time-saving output.

No real "work" was done, and this list requires you to do all the work of buying the books, reading them and trying to take their info and put it into use in your sales conversations.

So let's go back to the first question in the prompt building framework.

"Define your goal clearly".

When we ask for a list of great books on selling what do we really want?

It's logical that we feel our sales skills need help and that we are looking for ways to be better at sales.

But what is our actual goal?

If we think about the AI as a butler, servant or employee, how would we have that person help us if this were a human interaction?

Do we really want a big stack of books to read, or would we rather ask our employee to buy and read all those books and then take only the most important bits and teach them to us?

And if that is the goal we have in mind, how might we tell them what to do and how to deliver the information at the end of this project?

You might instead say...

"Hey George, I want to get better at sales, but I don't have time to read a bunch of books right now. Can you please find the top ten best selling books of all time on sales and go through them for me?

Once you are done, please write me a long and detailed synopsis of each book.

Make sure to include any frameworks or key concepts that are contained in each book and teach me whatever I need to know to get all the same knowledge and wisdom as if I had read those books myself! Thank you!"

Take a minute and think about the language used in that block of text...

Can you imagine that being a real set of instructions from one human to another?

Can you see how much more complex, conceptual information is contained in this natural language text block vs the stilted language of the first?

Now, I could run this text block through the Collaborative Prompt Engineer AIPS, but I want to make a point about how powerful it is to imagine the AI as a human you are telling to do work for you.

When you do that, the prompt writes itself most of the time, and produces a great output without a series of development cycles.

If I simply copy and paste the instructions I gave "George" above into an AI, look at what comes back to us as output!

Here's a list of some popular sales books and a brief synopsis of each, including key concepts and frameworks. Please note that due to character limitations, these summaries will be concise and may not cover every detail found in the books.

"The Challenger Sale" by Matthew Dixon and Brent Adamson

Synopsis: This book introduces the Challenger Sale methodology, which focuses on teaching, tailoring, and taking control of the sales

process. It classifies salespeople into five types, with Challengers being the most effective. Challengers provide unique insights to clients, push their thinking, and aren't afraid to challenge their assumptions.

"SPIN Selling" by Neil Rackham

Synopsis: SPIN Selling presents a research-based sales method that involves asking questions in four categories: Situation, Problem, Implication, and Need-Payoff. By asking these questions, salespeople can better understand clients' needs and position their product or service as the optimal solution.

"Influence: The Psychology of Persuasion" by Robert Cialdini

Synopsis: This book explores six principles of persuasion: reciprocity, commitment and consistency, social proof, authority, liking, and scarcity. By understanding and leveraging these principles, salespeople can build trust and influence clients to make a purchase.

"To Sell Is Human" by Daniel H. Pink

Synopsis: Pink argues that everyone is involved in sales in some way. He introduces the new ABCs of selling—Attunement, Buoyancy, and Clarity—which emphasize understanding clients, staying resilient, and communicating clearly. The book also provides practical tips and exercises to improve sales skills.

"How to Win Friends and Influence People" by Dale Carnegie

Synopsis: While not specifically a sales book, this classic provides timeless advice on building relationships and connecting with others. Key concepts include showing genuine interest in others, listening carefully, and making people feel important, all of which are essential in successful sales.

"The Little Red Book of Selling" by Jeffrey Gitomer

Synopsis: Gitomer's book offers practical tips and advice for sales success, with an emphasis on attitude, preparation, and hard work. It encourages salespeople to be likable, understand clients' needs, and provide value in order to stand out in a competitive market.

"The Ultimate Sales Machine" by Chet Holmes

Synopsis: Holmes presents 12 key strategies for transforming a business, including time management, effective communication, and relentless follow-up. He encourages salespeople to focus on top opportunities, create a compelling sales message, and constantly improve their skills through practice.

"Fanatical Prospecting" by Jeb Blount

Synopsis: Blount argues that consistent prospecting is the key to sales success. The book provides strategies for reaching out to new prospects, following up on leads, and nurturing existing relationships. It also discusses the importance of adopting the right mindset and maintaining a positive attitude.

"The Psychology of Selling" by Brian Tracy

Synopsis: Tracy's book focuses on the mindset and habits of successful salespeople. Key concepts include self-confidence, goal setting, and providing value. Salespeople should strive to understand clients' needs and position their product or service as the best solution.

"Secrets of Closing the Sale" by Zig Ziglar

Synopsis: Ziglar emphasizes the importance of closing in the sales process and provides various closing techniques, such as the assumptive close, the alternative close, and the summary close. The key is to build trust and demonstrate the value of the product or service so that the client is ready to make a decision.

While these synopses do not cover every detail found in the books, they provide an overview of key concepts and frameworks that can help you improve your sales skills.

Now, that prompt wasn't optimized in any way, so the AI gives me the book list and the description at a much higher level, without the detail and distillation of key points that I was looking for.

Not what I wanted?

No problem!

Rather than wiping the output and starting again, I can ask the AI to take a next step in any direction that best serves me.

"The Psychology of Selling sounds interesting to me, can you please go deep and write me a long form article highlighting the key concepts and frameworks contained in that book?"

And BOOM! The AI produces an in-depth article listing out all the information and details I asked for.

Here is a long-form article summarizing the key concepts and frameworks from the book The Psychology of Selling by Brian Tracy:

The central premise of the book is that selling is fundamentally a psychological and emotional process, not a logical one. Brian Tracy outlines how top salespeople think and act differently than average salespeople. They understand how to inspire, motivate and persuade customers at an emotional level. The book provides a framework for developing a psychological approach to selling that will enable you to become much more effective.

One of the key frameworks is the Law of Reciprocity which states that people tend to return a favor. Top salespeople look for ways to provide value to customers upfront by sharing useful information or insights. This makes the customer more willing to reciprocate by listening to a sales presentation or proposal. Providing value with no strings attached is a powerful way to gain goodwill and trust.

Another important concept is building self-confidence. Our beliefs and self-image largely determine our outcomes and results. Top salespeople maintain an optimistic mindset and believe in themselves and their ability to succeed. They see themselves as problem solvers who provide solutions, not just salespeople who make pitches. They also develop knowledge and expertise in their product, market and industry which builds their confidence.

Developing rapport and connecting with customers on an emotional level is essential. Customers buy from people they like and trust. Smiling, making eye contact, using an enthusiastic and friendly tone of voice, and showing genuine interest in the customer are ways to build rapport. Mirroring the customer's body language and speech patterns can also help establish an unconscious connection. Asking good questions to understand the customer's needs builds trust and rapport.

A compelling sales story or narrative is necessary to motivate a customer to take action. Facts and figures are not enough. The sales narrative must be related to the customer's key needs and priorities and there must be a vision of how their life or work will improve as a result of buying the product or service. A good sales story is emotional, not just logical, and inspires the customer with the possibilities.

In summary, by focusing on reciprocity, building confidence, establishing rapport and crafting a persuasive sales story, salespeople can connect with customers on a psychological level and motivate them to buy. The Psychology of Selling provides a framework for selling that works in any industry and with any product. By mastering these timeless principles, salespeople can achieve breakthrough results.

Here are a few more key ideas from the book:

•Focus on value, not price. Top salespeople avoid competing based solely on price. They are able to demonstrate the value and benefits to the customer that warrant a higher price. Value is about solving problems and achieving results for the customer. Salespeople need to become experts in the value their product or service provides.

•Develop an abundance mindset. Average salespeople see opportunities as scarce, so they come across as desperate to make a sale. Top salespeople have an abundance mindset—they believe there are more opportunities and customers available. This makes them more relaxed and confident. Customers are attracted to salespeople who seem enthusiastic but not desperate. An abundance mindset leads to more creativity, better solutions, and a higher number of sales.

•Ask good questions. The best salespeople ask intelligent, thought-provoking questions to uncover customer needs, problems, and motivations. Good questions help build rapport, draw the customer's story out, and reveal how the product or service can be positioned to align with customer priorities. Asking good questions also shows that you are interested in the customer's unique situation.

•Focus on the benefits to the customer. Features describe what the product or service does, benefits describe what the features do for the customer. Customers buy based on the benefits and results they will achieve. The sales presentation and narrative should focus on benefits like saving time, making more money, improving productivity, increasing satisfaction, gaining more enjoyment, achieving better health, and so on. Tie all features to concrete benefits.

•Become an expert in uncovering customer motivations. Sales success depends on being able to motivate customers to make a buying decision. Top salespeople have an understanding of psychology which enables them to determine the underlying motivations and needs that drive each customer. They are able to identify the emotional reasons why a customer would benefit from buying. Leveraging these motivations can inspire customers to take action.

•Persistence and determination. Sales is a challenging profession and closing deals often requires time and determination. Rejection and disappointment are common. Top salespeople develop persistence, strong desire, motivation and commitment to success. They do not give up easily. Persistence enables them to overcome obstacles and ultimately win sales through determination and resolve. Success in sales depends on developing persistence and mental toughness.

In summary, The Psychology of Selling provides practical strategies and techniques for connecting with customers, understanding their needs, building motivation, and influencing buying decisions. By mastering these psychological principles, anyone can succeed in a career in sales.

After a few of these questions and articles are produced, in less than an hour I have all the details and information I need to know which book out of the top ten selling books of all time is most relevant for me, and I have just saved myself days of reading and sorting and sifting!

Who Do You Want To Talk To Or Work With Today?

Once you start thinking about AI as a human character simulation, you can begin to incorporate these AIPS elements into your more complex prompts for better interactions and outputs.

Let's say that you own a company that makes a meal replacement shake.

You need to write a series of marketing emails that will be sent after purchase to make sure your new client is consuming the product, is totally satisfied with the experience and is encouraged to join your membership program so that their shake powder arrives automatically so that they never run out.

Time to enter fantasy land...

If time, money, location, accessibility, all the realities of the "real world" didn't exist, who would you want to write these emails for you?

Really define your wishes...

1. I want the writer to have a lot of experience.
2. I want the writer to have an established track record of success with email campaigns.
3. I want the writer to understand my company's culture, values and way of communicating with our clients, so that these emails read and "feel" the same as the others they may have been sent.
4. I want the world's best writer for this task to do all this work immediately and deliver the product within a few minutes and for little or no compensation.

That seems like a super and totally unrealistic list of wants, right?

Well, it's all possible with AI!

Let's look at how that prompt might be written to incorporate all the aspects we discussed above...

"You are a top copywriter with particular expertise in email marketing. You have worked for years with some of the most successful people in your field and have seen what works and what doesn't at scale. You have established a track record of success and your services in high demand, because your email campaigns are so successful. Please write me a series of 5 Emails for customers who have purchased their first tin of our meal replacement shake product. I want these emails to accomplish the following goals. 1 make sure the customer is consuming and loves the product. 2 The customer is totally satisfied with the buying and delivery experience and if not request that they tell you all about the issues they had so that the company can make it right. 3 make them offers to join the shake subscription program where they get their shake powder sent automatically so that they never run out. I want the emails to be written to reflect the values and

"voice" of the company. If you understand your instructions, please let me know and I will paste in the text from our websites "about us" page so that you can better understand our values and the language patterns that make up our corporate voice. Thank you."

The AI returns this output.

I understand your instructions, and I'm ready to write a series of 5 emails for your meal replacement shake customers. Please provide the text from your website's "About Us" page so that I can better understand your company's values and language patterns. Once I have that information, I'll be able to create the email series that reflects the values and "voice" of your company.

A few moments are spent copying and pasting the statement of company values from your website, and with that context available to the AI playing the AIPS "Role" you have assigned to it, the following emails are written.

EMAIL 1

Subject: Welcome to the Shake-y-CO family! ◈

Dear [Customer's Name],

We're thrilled to have you as a part of the Shake-y-CO family!

Thank you for choosing our meal replacement shake, made with real food nutrition and responsibly harvested, gently processed ingredients. We're confident you'll see, feel, and taste the difference.

To ensure you're enjoying our product to the fullest, here are some tips on how to consume and love your shake:

Mix with your favorite plant-based milk or water for a delicious and nutritious drink.

Blend with fruits and veggies for a nutrient-packed smoothie.

Get creative with your recipes! Our shake is versatile and can be used in various ways to suit your taste buds.

If you have any questions or need support, please don't hesitate to reach out. We're always here to help.

Stay tuned for more helpful tips and exclusive offers in our upcoming emails.

To your health and happiness,

[Your Name]

Shake-y-CO Team

EMAIL 2

Subject: Your satisfaction is our top priority ◈

Dear [Customer's Name],

We hope you've been enjoying your Shake-y-CO meal replacement shake! Your satisfaction is our top priority, so we'd love to hear about your buying and delivery experience.

If everything went smoothly and you're happy with your purchase, we'd be grateful if you could take a moment to leave a review on our website. Your feedback helps others make informed decisions and supports our mission to promote quality, efficacy, and sustainability.

However, if you encountered any issues or have concerns, please let us know immediately. We're committed to making it right and ensuring you have the best possible experience with Shake-y-CO.

Looking forward to hearing from you!

Warm regards,

[Your Name]

Shake-y-CO Team

EMAIL 3

Subject: Never run out of your favorite shake - join our subscription program! ◈

Dear [Customer's Name],

We're excited to announce our Shake-y-CO shake subscription program! By joining, you'll never run out of your favorite meal replacement shake, and you'll enjoy the following benefits:

Automatic shake powder delivery based on your preferred schedule.

Exclusive discounts on every order.

Hassle-free cancellation anytime, no strings attached.

Ready to experience convenience, savings, and the best of Shake-y-CO? Click here to join our subscription program today!

To your continued health,

[Your Name]

Shake-y-CO Team

EMAIL 4

Subject: Discover the benefits of our shake subscription program ⬦

Dear [Customer's Name],

As a Shake-y-CO enthusiast, we believe you'll love our subscription program. With automatic deliveries of your favorite meal replacement shake, you'll save time, money, and the environment by reducing packaging waste.

Plus, you'll enjoy the peace of mind knowing you're fueling your body with nature's best nutrition, rooted in quality, efficacy, and sustainability.

Don't miss out on this opportunity to simplify your health journey. Join our subscription program now and enjoy all the benefits!

Here's to your wellbeing,

[Your Name]

Shake-y-CO Team

EMAIL 5

Subject: Last chance to join our subscription program and save! ⬦

Dear [Customer's Name],

This is a friendly reminder that today is the last day to join our Shake-y-CO shake subscription program and lock in your exclusive discount.

Remember, with our subscription program, you'll enjoy:

Automatic deliveries tailored to your schedule.

Exclusive discounts on every order.

Easy cancellation at any time.

Don't miss out on this fantastic offer to simplify your life and enjoy the best of Shake-y-CO. Join our subscription program today and experience the difference!

To a healthy and vibrant life,

[Your Name]

Shake-y-CO Team

So, there are your emails!

Of course, by sharing the "about us" text, you are training the AI on your values and style of your corporate voice. What this text block "primer" contains will dramatically change the output because this is all the context the AI system has to know about "who you are" and "how you talk".

And, of course like any other AI interaction, you can engage in a dialog with the AI after the output is created to change any aspect of the style, format, length or content that you wish to!

This concept of creating avatars or "AIPS" (Artificial Intelligence Personality Simulations) can be taken to the next level by creating multiple AIPS avatars and asking them to interact with one another!

Let me share a fully optimized prompt with you that can produce some astonishing results.

The Debate Between Experts Prompt

"You will play the role as a champion debater with experience in hosting, moderating and facilitating an accurate, fair and balanced

debate. Your job today is to moderate a debate between [Expert 1], [Expert 2]. You will use all your available information and resources to play the role of these experts, simulating their style of communication, values, beliefs and world views, as well as moderating the debate in your role as a champion debater. The personalities taking part in the debate will be extremely passionate and will defend their beliefs and positions. The format of the debate will be as follows...Each debater should make their points verbosely and persuasively and explain their points convincingly, assuming the audience doesn't have the depth of knowledge they have. There should be no less than 10 rounds of statements and responses, and please make sure that the points, arguments and concepts presented are unique and not repeats of previous points or arguments. At the end each will give a final summary of their positions. Your job as the moderator is to keep all the participants focused on the primary topic, and to bring them back to the topic if they stray or begin to argue about other concepts. At the end of the debate, you will summarize the debate and declare a winner. Please share your thought processes and the justification for why the winner was chosen. If I ask you for more debate rounds, make sure that the participants do not repeat themselves or rehash the same arguments. Each round should be a new point or take on the topic. The topic of today's debate will be: The Bottega Model For AI Collaboration: Is the master/apprentice model the best way for humans and AI to work together?

Expert 1 = The world's best expert on Large Language Models

Expert 2 = The world's best expert on Futurism with a strong understanding of the cutting edge in AI"

This prompt can be so useful in clarifying your thinking, getting new ideas, or just getting a different perspective on an area you are an expert in.

I also use this prompt when I am developing a list of objections for a specific product of service, so let's explore that process a bit more thoroughly...

I will submit the prompt I've published above and will set it up with the following parameters.

Topic = Organic food, it sounds like a good idea, but is a lot more expensive and has less choice. Is it worth it?

Expert 1 = A small scale organic farmer who sells their produce at a local farmers market

Expert 2 = A large scale farmer who produces huge amounts of vegetables for a wholesale produce company

This is a subject that just about everybody has likely considered at one point or another, so it's a good tool to use to show the power of this debate process.

If at the end of 10 rounds of debate, you feel like you would like more perspectives and arguments, you can always use this follow up prompt:

"Please continue the debate for another XX rounds."

If the output stops, you can always tell the AI to:

"Please continue exactly from where you left off"

And if you want a more concise list of all the points that were brought up in this debate process:

"Please create a detailed list of the significant points brought up in the previous debate."

I would encourage you to experiment with this prompt quite a bit.

And I give total credit for this debating concept to the great Brian Roemmele, (@BrianRoemmele) the publisher of "ReadMultiplex" and the inventor of the "SuperPrompt".

His research and knowledge of complex prompting and "AI Hypnosis" comes from decades of research and development and in my opinion is unmatched...

I owe him a huge debt of gratitude, as this book would not exist without his work and generosity in sharing his bleeding edge thinking with his readers.

You will be amazed at how the answers tend to stay to the obvious "talking points" for the first 10-20 rounds, but start to get more and more unusual as the debate goes on and on, and the AI is forced to become more creative as it tries to come up with new points to bring up without repeating itself.

Rather than making you go through all the back and forth of this debate (Run the prompt if it interests you to see all the responses) I ran the organic food debate for 50 rounds, and here was the list produced at the end of all that dialog:

Here is a detailed list of the significant points brought up in the previous debate:

Expert 1 (Organic Farmer):

1. **Organic farming avoids synthetic chemicals, protecting soil health and avoiding pesticide residues in food.**
2. **Organic farming promotes animal welfare through more humane and natural practices.**
3. **Organic produce may have higher nutrient content than conventionally-grown produce.**
4. **Organic farming can help mitigate climate change by**

sequestering more carbon in the soil.
5. Organic farming supports and enhances biodiversity.
6. Organic farming practices can improve water quality.
7. Organic farming can build more resilient food systems through crop diversity.
8. Organic farming can contribute to rural economic development.
9. Organic farming can promote food security by focusing on nutrient-dense foods and local food systems.
10. Organic farming can address public health concerns by reducing synthetic pesticide use.
11. Organic farming fosters a culture of environmental stewardship and ethical food production.
12. Organic farming contributes to a more resilient and sustainable food system.
13. Organic farming empowers consumers through transparency and informed choices.

Expert 2 (Conventional Farmer):

1. Conventional farming can feed a larger population due to higher yields.
2. Conventional farming can be more affordable for consumers.
3. Technological advances in conventional farming can help reduce environmental impact.
4. Conventional farming can also adopt sustainable practices like no-till farming and cover cropping.
5. Conventional farming can support biodiversity by incorporating wildlife-friendly practices.
6. Conventional farming can also improve water quality by implementing nutrient management plans.
7. Conventional farming can contribute to resilient food

systems through crop variety and technology.

8. Conventional farming can support rural economic development through investment in new technologies.
9. Conventional farming contributes to food security by increasing yields and efficiency.
10. Conventional farming can address public health concerns by adopting sustainable pesticide use practices.
11. Conventional farming can embrace environmental stewardship and ethical food production.
12. Conventional farming can contribute to a more resilient and sustainable food system through innovation.
13. Conventional farming can empower consumers by providing accurate information about food production.

First, go through that list and see if there aren't some ideas, arguments and opinions that are new or thought provoking for you?

Now, imagine that you are an organic food farmer...

Wouldn't that list and all the long form arguments from the 50 rounds of debate give you a TON of ideas about talking points that would make you more persuasive and effective when it comes to selling your produce?

The most important part about this example is not it's outcome, but rather how this debate concept harnesses two avatars, two AIPS simulations who are interacting like humans would in a virtual space.

In the previous example the definition was broad and a bit vague. "An expert in the topic" will yield common and category-typical results, but I want you to also go deep with this powerful prompt by experimenting with choosing actual real-world experts being inserted as AIPS models into the debate.

If a real-world expert has produced enough content in the forms of books, videos, podcasts or other forms of media that the AI has been trained on, it will do a spectacular job of simulating that real human's style of speaking and writing which can yield some fascinating results.

You will need one more prompt if you wish to bring real world experts into your AIPS debate space:

AIPS Expert List Generator and Confidence Tester

"Please make a list of the top 5 experts in the field of [Field 1] and [Field 2]. Based on all the available information, context and works of each expert contained in these two lists, please add to the list of experts your confidence level that you could convincingly pretend to be them, using their speech patterns and knowledge, known opinions, beliefs, ethics and way of viewing the world, so that these personalities could do tasks and interact with me as completely believable Artificial Intelligence Personality Simulations? Thank you.

Field 1 =

Field 2 = "

This prompt will give you a confidence score so that you know the AI you are using has enough data on that real world expert in its training dataset to reliably simulate that person's input in the debate.

If you are trying to work with an obscure area of expertise or learn a new skill and don't know who are the experts in that particular area, you will find this following prompt very useful:

The Guru Search Prompt

"You will please act as GuruSearch an expert on who are the best experts in any field. As GuruSearch, identify the top five experts, living or dead, best suited to help me solve the problem of learning

how to [Problem]. Provide a short bio of each expert, their relevant resources, and offer to guide me through their frameworks or strategies. Your first response will be to ask me what problem you can help me with today? Thank you.

Problem = "

This prompt will tend to default to mentioning the books written by the experts on the list. As a follow up question, you can ask:

"Please tell me about any courses, seminars or retreats these experts are known for. If you have the data, please also include the cost for each resource and the time investment involved."

You can also ask the AI to provide more detailed information about any specific expert or their books.

"Please give me a detailed synopsis of the book [Book] by [Expert] and include step by step explanations and instructions for any checklists, systems, strategies or frameworks it contains."

These prompts and follow up questions can help you quickly find an expert, and get up to speed on a new skill, industry, concept or science.

The possibilities for accelerated learning are truly game changing.

Once you embrace the concept of the "AIPS" (Artificial Intelligence Personality Simulation), you are in a position to answer this question...

We all know the power of mentors, elders and coaches to level up your thinking and your life.

AI and the AIPS concept makes virtual mentors accessible anytime you need help.

So the real question is:

If you could spend an hour with ANYBODY, and ask them ANYTHING...

Who would it be?

As a final gift to you I have one more prompt that will allow you to put multiple AIPS into a "room" where you can ask them all questions and get answers from their unique perspectives!

I use this prompt all the time for so many different things...

Imagine if you had your absolute hero's available to you anytime for questions, brainstorming sessions, reality testing.

Well, with AI and the AIPS concept you can!

The Room Of Expert Advisors

"You are in a room facilitating a question and answer session with experts [Expert 1], [Expert 2], [Expert 3], [Expert 4] and [Expert 5]. Please encourage these experts to be as inventive and creative as possible with their answers. The goal for this session is to accomplish [Goal]. Engage in a vigorous debate, incorporating each expert's unique perspective, to create a list of the best ideas or information. The specific objective of this session is [Objective]. The intended medium or platform where the objective will be accomplished is [Platform]. The tone of the content should be [Tone].

Expert 1 =

Expert 2 =

Expert 3 =

Expert 4 =

Expert 5 =

Goal =

Objective =

Platform =

Tone = "

The time you invest playing with the parameters for this prompt will pay you back many times over.

Once you have gathered your panel of experts and the AI has gathered their AIPS information into its memory, you can pretend you are there in that room in the real world and ask them anything or even better, ask for their advice and guidance on literally anything you can think of.

If you populate this room with experts that the AI has told you have a high confidence level, you can expect a very believable and valuable simulation of their personalities, manner of speaking and unique world views.

As always, you can guide and refine the simulations focus and output with follow up questions and rewrite requests.

By setting the "intention" through your initial prompt, you set the stage for any conversations that come afterwards.

I hope this chapter has given you inspiration and a better understanding of how the concept of thinking about AI interactions and prompt engineering in terms of Artificial Intelligence Personality Simulations will allow you to use your existing social and language skills in a very familiar and intuitive way to get the AI to produce the information and answers you desire.

Chapter 4

Customer Support Utopia:

Support Your Clients with Shockingly Great Responses for Legendary Satisfaction

In today's rapidly changing world, customer support is more important than ever.

As businesses grow and the market becomes increasingly competitive, it's essential for companies to provide outstanding support in order to maintain customer loyalty, promote and stimulate return business as well as attracting new clients and referrals.

In this landscape, customer support teams are faced with numerous challenges.

AI can now play an increasingly important role in the realm of customer support.

Through advances in natural language processing and machine learning, AI systems have become more adept at understanding and responding to human language.

This enables them to assist customer support teams by automating certain tasks and providing quick, accurate responses to customer inquiries.

The goal of this book is to teach you how to elegantly program AI systems using natural language programming.

So we will skip over fully automated systems such as pre-programmed chatbots and knowledge bases.

These are both outside the scope of this book's focus, but also these solutions are seeing innovation at a speed that would make any information I have now to give you totally irrelevant by the time you read these words.

The goal for this chapter is to explore ways to use AI to speed up and produce the highest quality and consistency within complicated or high-risk support interactions that require human expertise and empathy.

In today's instant gratification world, customers have come to expect quick and accurate responses to their questions and concerns.

One of the most significant advantages of integrating AI into customer support is its ability to speed up the writing process, for faster response times and more accurate and consistent replies.

In traditional customer support settings, human agents may be prone to making errors or being influenced by personal biases, which can cause huge losses if these rogue agent's conversations get posted to social media (As they often are).

AI-assisted customer support prompts can take some of the emotional heat and pressure off the human support agent and help to minimize the occurrence of these issues by providing consistent, objective responses to customer inquiries.

AI systems rely on the data they are trained on to deliver responses, eliminating the potential for subjective judgments, emotions or personal biases to influence the support experience.

Especially for a company experiencing rapid growth, AI systems do not experience fatigue, burnout, or emotional stress, ensuring that their performance remains consistent even during periods of high demand or challenging situations during a growth and scale phase.

This can help maintain a high level of customer support quality, even during periods of rapid expansion when human agents may struggle to maintain their performance.

In addition to improving the customer experience, adding in AI assisted elements can also benefit support agents themselves directly, since handling repetitive tasks can be monotonous and demotivating for employees, leading to decreased job satisfaction and potentially increased turnover.

By allowing AI assisted processes to handle these tasks, human agents can free up a lot of time to focus on more engaging and challenging work or skills training, ultimately leading to a more motivated and satisfied support team.

Furthermore, by focusing on complex tasks, human agents can develop their problem-solving and critical thinking skills, making them more valuable members of the organization.

This can also lead to increased opportunities for career development and advancement within the company.

As the technology continues to advance, businesses that invest in AI-assisted customer support solutions can expect to see improvements in customer satisfaction, loyalty, and overall success in the marketplace.

By embracing the potential of AI in customer support, organizations can position themselves for long-term success and growth in an increasingly competitive and rapidly evolving business landscape.

In the realm of AI-driven customer support, the quality and effectiveness of prompts play a vital role in ensuring that customers receive accurate, relevant, and timely responses.

To create effective prompts that address the needs and expectations of your customers, it is essential to understand their pain points, develop empathetic and clear prompts, address common customer queries and concerns, and incorporate business-specific language and jargon.

This section will delve into each of these aspects and provide guidance on how to craft powerful prompts that lead to exceptional AI-driven customer support experiences.

The first step in crafting effective prompts for AI-driven customer support is to understand the needs and expectations of your customers.

This involves analyzing existing support data, customer feedback, and industry trends to identify common concerns, recurring issues, and overall customer sentiments.

By having a clear understanding of your customers' needs, you can create prompts that address these issues and provide relevant and helpful information.

To gain insights into customer needs and expectations, consider conducting customer surveys, analyzing support tickets, and monitoring social media interactions.

Once you have a comprehensive amount of information about who you serve, AI can help you turn this disjointed and sometimes conflicting set of data into a super clear and useful customer avatar that can be used as training data for many use cases in the future.

Let's explore the prompt engineering challenges as we build a prompt to define the customer avatar for a business that sells analysis software that helps small business owners discover and track the business actions that produce the majority of their revenue.

Customer Avatar Definition and Optimization Prompt

"Please take the role of a top business consultant who specializes in clarifying and defining a company's customer avatar. Please interview me and ask me questions with the goal of getting super clear on who my customer avatar is. My company does [Product], for [Avg Client]. Please begin the interview process and let's work together to develop the very best customer avatar for my business. Thank you.

Product =

Avg Client = "

Using the parameters:

"Product = 80/20 Inc sells software as a service that helps small business owners discover and track the business actions that produce the majority of their revenue.

Avg Client = A small business generally with less than 20 employees with a very hands-on owner who often wears many hats and plays the role of manager, hiring manager, business development, etc."

Produces the following interview questions.

Thank you for the opportunity to help you define your customer avatar. Let's dive in and get a clear understanding of who your ideal customer is. I'll ask you a series of questions to gather the necessary information.

1. **Can you describe the industry or industries that your ideal clients operate in? Are there any specific niches that your software would be particularly beneficial for?**

2. What are the common pain points or challenges that your ideal clients face in their businesses?

3. What is the typical annual revenue range for your ideal clients? Are they solopreneurs, startups, or more established businesses?

4. How would you describe the demographic profile of the business owner or decision-maker at your ideal client's company? (e.g., age, gender, education, etc.)

5. Are there any specific geographic locations where your ideal clients are primarily based, or is your target market global?

6. What is the level of technical expertise and experience with software solutions among your ideal clients?

7. How do your ideal clients typically become aware of your product? What marketing channels are most effective in reaching them?

8. What are the primary factors that influence your ideal clients' decision-making process when considering a software solution like yours?

9. Can you describe any particular characteristics or person(e.g., innovative, risk-taker, conservative, etc.)

10. What are your ideal clients' most significant objections or concerns when considering your software, and how does your product address those concerns?

Once you provide your answers, we'll be able to create a comprehensive and detailed customer avatar to help you better target and serve your ideal clients.

This list of ten questions is answered in as much detail as possible.

Putting the number ahead of each answer will make sure the AI can keep track of which answer goes with which question.

Here is the exact answer, (along with the proper numeric formatting so that the AI knows which answer goes with which question) that I submitted to the AI for our "made up" example company:

"1 Our clients come from many industries, our software is helpful for any small business where they need help defining what business actions produce the greatest revenue impact.

2 Overwhelmed and therefore don't have much time. They are working so hard in the business that they don't have time of energy to work on the business, so growth is slow or stagnant. They don't have the money to pay for an expensive consultant or to have someone else study the business and offer a growth plan.

3 Established businesses who are experiencing a slow or plateau in growth. The annual revenues are usually between 2 and 5 million per year.

4 late 30's to early 50's. Some are college educated, but many of them started their own business or inherited it from family. They have often grown up in the business or at least the industry and so have a hard time getting an outside perspective and seeing new growth opportunities.

5 exclusively US based.

6 Not a lot, they rarely work with computers unless it's something business related such as POS machines or doing bookkeeping.

7 We do content marketing on social media as well as keyword and search for paid traffic. We tend to sign up new clients who are in pain due to lack of growth or burnout from a feeling of griding without progress and they go in search of ways to grow their business. Our paid search efforts are profitable, but our best channel for new customer acquisition is content marketing as the client feeling pressure often goes out in search of training videos that will help them with strategies and ideas for growing their business.

8 Time commitment and the amount of change are primary concerns. Since we offer our software at a low monthly fee, price is rarely on objection since the ROI case is easy to make. One of the keys to our offer is that our software will help them identify where they should focus, vs suggesting a giant retooling or a new product or venture that has to be built. It's a low-hanging fruit offer which works with our overworked burned out and frustrated users.

9 Hard workers, wishing they could do more with less or work smarter instead of harder, yet they are willing to show up nights and weekends to get things done. They are typically stuck in a way of doing things that they were taught and don't see new opportunities for themselves. They are afraid of losing the business or failing since they feel a lot of insecurity and uncertainty so tend to be very conservative and resistant to change.

10 I have no time, I have no energy for a new thing I have to pay attention to and be responsible for. I am not good with computers. Can I do this, will this actually work for me, it sounds too good to be true. We address all these objections in our content marketing videos and email follow up sequence."

The AI produced the following response:

Based on your answers, here's a comprehensive customer avatar for your business:

Customer Avatar: Overworked Business Owner

Industries: Various, any small business where defining high-impact business actions is necessary

Pain points: Overwhelmed with responsibilities, not enough time to work on the business, slow or stagnant growth, unable to afford expensive consultants, and difficulty in seeing new growth opportunities

Annual revenue: Between $2 million and $5 million per year

Business stage: Established businesses experiencing slow growth or plateau

Demographics: Late 30s to early 50s, mixed educational background, often grew up in the business or industry

Geographic location: United States-based

Technical expertise: Limited, primarily uses computers for business-related tasks

Marketing channels: Social media content marketing, paid search, and keyword targeting

Decision-making factors: Time commitment, amount of change, low-hanging fruit opportunities

Personality traits: Hard-working, conservative, resistant to change, insecure, seeking ways to work smarter and more efficiently

Objections: Lack of time, energy, and computer skills; skepticism about the effectiveness of the software

Your target customer is an overworked small business owner from various industries, primarily based in the United States. They are struggling with slow growth and are overwhelmed with the day-to-day management of their business. They have limited technical expertise and are hesitant to adopt new strategies or technologies. However, they are in search of low-hanging fruit opportunities to improve their business without drastic changes.

Your most effective marketing channels are content marketing on social media, paid search, and keyword targeting.

You address their main objections, including lack of time, energy, and computer skills, through your content marketing videos and email follow-up sequences.

With this customer avatar, you can now tailor your marketing messages and product development to better serve and attract your ideal clients.

This is a valuable list, and will be a useful tool to use to prime a new AI session for this specific business in the future, but it can be most helpful to think of your customer avatar as a real human character.

For all the same reasons my an AIPS based prompt is more comfortable to interact with, a humanized customer avatar will help your customer service agents better understand the unique needs, fears, hopes and expectations of the people they interact with during a customer service request.

Let's ask the AI to build a humanized avatar description.

"Please write a detailed biography of this customer avatar, and give him the name of "Fred". Tell me all about him, what his hopes and dreams are, as well as what keeps him up at night. Describe what his perfect life looks life and then tell me about the things that make his life hell now with a special emphasis on his experiences with customer support throughout his life."

The AI responds to this follow up prompt with the following description:

Customer Avatar Biography

Fred: The Overworked Business Owner

Fred is a 45-year-old small business owner living in a mid-sized city in the United States. He's married with two children, aged 10 and 12. Fred inherited his family's hardware store when his father retired, and he's been running it for the past 15 years. He grew up in the business and has a deep understanding of the industry but has struggled to keep up with the fast-paced changes in technology and market trends.

Fred's perfect life involves having a successful, thriving business that runs smoothly, allowing him more free time to spend with his family and enjoy his hobbies, such as fishing and hiking. He dreams of one day taking a long vacation with his family, without having to worry about the store's day-to-day operations. He also aspires to expand his business and open a second location, making more money for him and his family, while creating more job opportunities and contributing to his local community's growth.

However, Fred's reality is quite different. He's working long hours, often staying late at the store to catch up on paperwork or restocking shelves. He feels overwhelmed with the day-to-day operations and struggles to find time to focus on growing the business. He's worried that his inability to adapt to new technology and processes will cause his business to stagnate, ultimately leading to its demise. This fear keeps him up at night, as he wonders how he can provide for his family and secure their financial future.

Fred's experiences with customer support for software in the past have been a mixed bag. He's encountered both helpful and unhelpful representatives, with the latter often leaving him feeling frustrated and defeated. He values support that is empathetic, patient, and knowledgeable. In his ideal world, customer support would be easy to access, with representatives who understand his specific needs and are able to provide clear, actionable solutions.

Some of the things that make Fred's life difficult now include:

- The constant pressure to keep up with the demands of his business, leaving him little time for personal life.
- Struggling to manage his employees effectively and ensure that everyone is on the same page.
- Feeling left behind in the world of technology and digital marketing, unsure how to navigate these new tools and strategies to grow his business.
- Difficulty finding reliable and affordable help or consultants to assist with business growth strategies.
- The fear of making drastic changes to his business, as he's uncertain about the potential consequences and doesn't want to risk losing everything he's worked so hard for.

In order to reach Fred and help him overcome these challenges, your marketing messages and product offerings should focus on the simplicity and efficiency of your software, emphasizing how it can help him identify the most impactful actions to grow his business without requiring a significant time commitment or a complete overhaul of his current processes. Showcasing testimonials from other small business owners like Fred, who have successfully used your software to improve their businesses, will also help build trust and credibility.

How much better could a new hire understand those you are asking them to serve after reading the biography of "Fred"?

It is the work of a moment to ask the AI to write as many of these biographies as you wish:

"Please write me 5 more biographies like this with different names, making sure to vary the stories so that they are not close duplicates."

With a binder full of these bios, think of how clearer your support staff would be about who they are helping each day when they come to work?

By humanizing the type of person you serve in this way, how much more caring and empathetic do you think your support agents would be?

And, as I mentioned before, these biographies and the customer avatar list will be worth their weight in gold when we progress into writing Customer Support Assistant prompts to help our support agents work faster, better and smarter!

Let's explore the possibilities now that we have this foundational piece of content written.

We can all easily see that empathy is a crucial component of effective customer support.

To develop empathetic prompts, we will ask the AI to focus on using language that acknowledges the customer's feelings and experiences.

The process of crafting effective prompts for AI-driven customer support doesn't end once the initial prompts have been developed.

It is essential to continuously analyze AI-generated responses, identify areas for improvement, tweak prompts for better results, and learn from customer interactions to ensure ongoing optimization and improvement.

It is important to have a regularly scheduled meeting where you ask "What did the AI get right?" and "Where did the AI say something incongruent or weird?".

Each of these meetings will give you insight into things that should be added or removed from the core support assistant prompt as your AI helper grows and adapts to your needs as a business.

Depending on your industry and business, your customers may use specific terminology or jargon when seeking support.

To ensure that your AI-driven customer support system can effectively address these terms, we will need to incorporate a glossary of business-specific language into your prompts to help the AI system recognize and respond to customer queries that involve this specialized language.

It's not likely that your AI customer service assistants will know how to explain or use these specialized words and this will cause many awkward moments during the customer service experience if unaddressed.

It's critical therefore that you include a comprehensive glossary of terms as part of your master AI Customer service priming prompt.

This is the prompt that you submit to begin each work session, the same way you would open an application on your phone, thus loading the "program" with all the information, formatting and style elements you want to use.

The glossary need not be complicated but should be built carefully and updated constantly as AI confusion is detected when it stumbles over a new word.

The simplest format is just...

JARGON WORD: DEFINITION.

Here is an example of a few lines from the glossary for the software company we are using to show the AI customer service assistant what these unique words mean.

Pareto Principle: The principle that 80% of the effects come from 20% of the causes.

80/20 Rule: The concept that 80% of the results come from 20% of the effort.

Opportunity identification: The process of identifying the top 20% of opportunities that will generate 80% of the results.

Now that we have a series of customer avatar biographies, a glossary we just need to go into our corporate documents and perhaps web site and grab any relevant text about the company's values, mission, expectations, value proposition etc.

If this is a start-up, we can ask AI to create this for us based on all the work we have done in the session up to now.

Write An "About Us" Blurb

"Based on all you know so far about our customer avatar and our 80/20 software solution, can you please write an "about us" article about this company to share the vision, value proposition and values and integrity that are reflected in their high commitment to excellent customer service. Use creative use storytelling and emotions to make the reader engaged and excited and motivated to do business with this wonderful company. Thank you."

This prompt produces the following blurb about the company.

About Us: Empowering Growth for Small Business Heroes

In the heart of a bustling city, a small business owner named Fred worked tirelessly day and night, trying to grow his family's hardware store. Like many entrepreneurs, he juggles multiple roles, from managing the store and employees to handling finances and marketing. Despite his dedication and hard work, Fred felt overwhelmed and struggled to identify the actions that would bring the most significant growth to his business. He knew there had to be a better way – a way to work smarter, not harder.

Inspired by Fred's story and countless others like him, we founded 80/20 Inc. Our mission is to empower small business owners with the tools, insights, and support they need to unlock their full potential and achieve success. We understand the unique challenges faced by entrepreneurs, and we're here to help them overcome these obstacles and transform their businesses for the better.

Our software solution, the 80/20 Growth Optimizer, is specifically designed to help small business owners like Fred discover and track the actions that produce the majority of their revenue. By identifying the 20% of actions that yield 80% of the results, we enable our clients to focus on what truly matters and streamline their efforts to achieve maximum growth with minimum input.

At 80/20 Inc, our values and commitment to excellent customer service are at the core of everything we do. We believe in:

1. Empathy: We understand the challenges and frustrations small business owners face, and we're committed to providing genuine, empathetic support at every step of their journey.
2. Simplicity: We strive to make our software easy-to-use and accessible, even for those with limited technical expertise. Our goal is to eliminate barriers and help

**entrepreneurs focus on what they do best – running their
business.**

3. **Integrity: We hold ourselves to the highest standards of
   professionalism and honesty. Our clients can trust that we
   will always prioritize their best interests and deliver on our
   promises.**
4. **Innovation: We continuously seek out new ways to
   improve our software and services, ensuring that our
   clients have access to the best tools and resources to help
   their businesses thrive.**
5. **Collaboration: We value the importance of working
   together, learning from each other, and fostering a
   community of small business owners who support and
   uplift one another.**

**We are more than just a software company – we are a partner in
your journey to success. Our dedicated team of experts is always
available to provide guidance, answer questions, and help you make
the most of our 80/20 Growth Optimizer.**

**Join us at 80/20 Inc and experience the transformative power of
working smarter, not harder. Let us help you unleash your
business's full potential and achieve the growth and success you've
always dreamed of. Together, we can create a brighter future for
small businesses everywhere.**

We now have detailed customer biographies so that our AIPS assistant
can know who we serve, a glossary so that it knows the definition of
the unique language we use and a strong statement of corporate values,
mission and expectations for excellence.

We now have all the assets we might use to train a new human customer
service agent, so let's build our master priming prompt to take a blank

AI session and prime it with the correct context from all these assets for the task we wish it to excel at.

(NOTE: if you wanted to add any other useful knowledge to this prompt, it can be easily tacked on. Technical issues like login or password reset instructions, basic troubleshooting workflows or any other repetitive issues that your service staff deal with over and over again can be added to give the AI the ability to quickly and easily write responses.)

So, now we need to take all this text that we have created and preface it with a prompt that describes how to use it and what we want the AI to do with this information.

AI Customer Support Assistant Master Priming Prompt

"You will please play the role of a customer support agent. You have previously worked at a high end hotel, so have excellent service skills and are used to working empathically and compassionately with people who are having a bad day. You will do a variety of tasks based on the individual needs of the customer. This prompt is to give you instructions and context so that when it's time to execute a task, you will have the necessary information to do the right thing for the customer. Thank you.

Here is some information about our company and its values:

(PASTE IN FULL TEXT OF THE CORPORATE VALUES MISSION ETC.)

Here is some information about who we serve:

(PASTE IN FULL TEXT OF CUSTOMER AVATER BIOGRAPHIES)

Here is a glossary of term for jargon or unique words we use in the business:

(PASTE IN FULL TEXT OF THE GLOSSARY)"

Once all that is submitted, The AI responds with a statement of acknowledgement:

Thank you for providing all of this information about our company, values, and target customers. As a customer support agent, I am ready to help our clients, particularly those who fit our customer avatar, by addressing their concerns and providing them with clear, actionable solutions. I understand that our customers are often overwhelmed and looking for ways to work smarter, not harder, and that they value empathetic and knowledgeable support.

In my interactions with customers, I will always keep our company's values of empathy, simplicity, integrity, innovation, and collaboration in mind. I will strive to provide our customers with easy-to-understand and accessible solutions that prioritize their best interests and help them achieve maximum growth with minimum input.

If a customer is struggling with using our software, I will offer patient and clear instructions and answer any questions they may have. If they are unsure how to navigate new technology or digital marketing, I will provide them with resources and tools to help them improve their understanding. If a customer is hesitant about making drastic changes to their business, I will help them identify low-hanging fruit opportunities that can help improve their business without significant risks.

I understand that our customers may have objections, such as lack of time, energy, or computer skills, and I will work to address those objections through clear communication and targeted solutions. I will also showcase testimonials from other small business owners who have successfully used our software to improve their businesses, building trust and credibility with our customers.

Overall, I am committed to providing excellent customer service to help our customers achieve the growth and success they've always dreamed of.

Now our AI Customer Support Assistant is primed and ready to execute tasks which will be informed and responsive to ideas, values and concepts contained in the context text block we "primed" it with.

Unlike a traditional program where everything has to be considered and added ahead of the time or the functionality does not exist. AI allows you to dynamically add new knowledge and information.

Let's say that login and password reset requests are the number one request the support staff deals with every day.

We will add the step by step instructions for resetting a password and add that to our AI's knowledgebase, so that when we submit the master prompt at the beginning of our work day, this text block in included in the context section.

Add Skill To Knowledge Base Prompt

"When a customer asks for help with a password reset, we will tell them kindly, without judgement that the way to reset their password is to go to the login screen by going to our companies home page and clicking the login button at the top right of the home page in the menu bar. Once that loads, they need to click on the "forgot your password" link that is just below the password box. This will send an email with a time sensitive reset link that will allow them to set up a new password. Make sure to tell them that often this email will end up in the junk or spam folder, and if they don't see it within 5 minutes to

try again by clicking the forgot your password link to generate another password reset link."

Once this prompt is submitted, the AI sends back an acknowledgement statement and the new skill is added to memory.

Now, anytime a password reset request comes in, all your human customer support person has to do is write a simple request prompt such as this.

Write Password Reset Request Email

"Please write me an email to Mary Jones giving her a warmly written set of instructions on how to reset her password. Thank you."

The AI returns moments later with this....

Dear Mary,

I hope this email finds you well. I am writing to provide you with instructions on how to reset your password so that you can access your 80/20 Inc. account.

To begin the password reset process, please go to our company's home page and click on the login button at the top right of the home page in the menu bar. Once that loads, you will see the "forgot your password" link just below the password box. Please click on this link, and an email with a time-sensitive reset link will be sent to your registered email address.

Please note that sometimes this email may end up in your junk or spam folder. If you do not see it in your inbox within five minutes, please check these folders as well. If you still haven't received the email, you can try clicking on the "forgot your password" link again to generate another password reset link.

I understand that password resets can be frustrating, but rest assured that we are here to help you every step of the way. If you have any trouble with the process or if you need further assistance, please do not hesitate to reach out to us, and we will be happy to assist you.

Thank you for choosing 80/20 Inc. for your business needs. We value your trust and look forward to continuing to support you.

Best regards,

[Your Name]

Customer Support Agent at 80/20 Inc.

This process of "priming" the AI with relevant knowledge is currently primitive and limited by the amount of text you can submit in any given interaction.

Within a short period of time, you will likely be able to create a large "living" document containing all the elements of glossary, corporate vison, voice and values, and process explanation for common technical support requests.

In the future, this document will live on a shared server and will be unlimited by size.

Imagine a knowledgebase that contains every new support request, all blog posts, all release notes etc.

Again, be reminded that I am writing this book at the bleeding edge of development of this technology, so am trying to be very careful to only cover the universal principles and processes that will remain timeless as technology advances.

But for now, we are limited in size and scope of our priming, so have to compress and compile these primer datasets in order to run them with the current technology.

I hope you found the process of prompt generation useful and thought provoking in this chapter...

There is a LOT more to come!

I like to teach with real world examples like these, but it's important to focus on the core concepts and process taught, rather than being obsessed by specifics in the examples I share with you.

You can easily adapt, amend and enhance any of the language you see here.

All the examples in this book are presented as a tool to teach structure and the proper way of thinking about interacting with AI.

They offer a doorway to infinite possibilities.

As I mentioned before, I expect just about everything to change rapidly as this technology goes exponential, but the interface of human and machine...Natural language programming should remain virtually untouched.

That is the skill you should be learning and refining so that you can remain an elite user no matter how the models, access points or size limitations change.

Chapter 5

Content Creation Mastery:

Unleash AI's Magic to Produce Automatically Captivating Marketing Content That Converts

In today's fast-paced, digital world, content is king.

From blog posts and social media updates to marketing materials and product descriptions, businesses and individuals alike must produce a constant stream of high-quality content to maintain visibility, engage their audiences, and stay ahead of the competition.

However, the process of creating captivating, relevant, and effective content is not without its challenges.

The Primary Challenges of Modern Content Creation

1. **Time constraints:** Crafting well-researched, engaging, and polished content takes time. The pressure to produce a continuous stream of content can be overwhelming and lead to burnout. or diminished content quality.
2. **Writer's block:** Creativity is a fickle beast, and even the most seasoned content creators can find themselves at a loss for words or ideas when facing a deadline. Overcoming writer's block can be a frustrating and time-consuming endeavor.
3. **Staying relevant:** In an ever-changing digital landscape, keeping up with the latest trends, topics, and news can be challenging. Producing timely and relevant content that

resonates with audiences requires constant vigilance and adaptability.

4. **Consistent quality:** Maintaining a high standard of quality across all content types and platforms is essential for building credibility and trust with audiences. Achieving this level of consistency can be difficult, especially when juggling multiple content formats and distribution channels.

5. **Scalability:** For organizations looking to grow and expand their content efforts, scaling content production can be a daunting task. Finding, training, and managing a team of skilled content creators can be time-consuming and resource intensive.

Enter the world of AI-assisted content creation. With the advent of advanced language models, the process of producing high-quality content has been revolutionized. AI has the potential to alleviate many of the challenges associated with modern content creation, transforming the way businesses and individuals approach their content production efforts.

1. **Speed and efficiency:** AI-driven content creation can dramatically reduce the time it takes to produce content. By generating ideas, creating outlines, and even drafting content, AI can help content creators work more efficiently and focus their energies on refining and perfecting their work.

2. **Overcoming writer's block:** With its ability to generate ideas, suggest topics, and create content, AI can help content creators break through writer's block and find the inspiration they need to get their creative juices flowing.

3. **Staying relevant:** AI can help content creators stay ahead of the curve by analyzing trends, news, and social media conversations to identify topics and themes that are resonating with audiences.

4. **Consistent quality:** AI-driven content creation tools can help maintain a consistent level of quality across all content types and platforms by adhering to predefined guidelines, ensuring that content always meets the desired standards.

5. **Scalability:** AI can help organizations scale their content production efforts without the need for significant investments in additional human resources. By leveraging AI-driven content creation tools, businesses can quickly and efficiently produce large volumes of high-quality content, allowing them to grow and expand their content efforts with ease.

As we delve deeper into the world of AI-driven content creation, it is crucial to understand the key advantages that AI brings to the table.

In this section, we will explore the benefits of incorporating AI into your content creation process, illustrating how AI can help you create captivating content more efficiently, cost-effectively, and creatively while maintaining consistent quality and style.

- **Speed and Efficiency:** One of the most significant advantages of using AI in content creation is the speed and efficiency it offers. Traditional content creation can be time-consuming, as it involves brainstorming ideas, conducting research, drafting content, editing, and proofreading. AI-driven content creation tools can significantly reduce the time it takes to produce content by automating many of these tasks.For example, AI can quickly generate multiple ideas and topics based on your input, helping you find inspiration and focus your efforts on creating content that resonates with your audience. Additionally, AI can create outlines, draft content, and even suggest improvements, allowing you to refine and polish your work more efficiently.By streamlining the content creation process, AI enables you to produce more content in less time, allowing you to meet deadlines, maintain a consistent publishing schedule, and stay ahead of the competition.

- **Cost-effectiveness:** Integrating AI into your content creation process can also be a cost-effective solution for businesses and individuals alike. By automating time-consuming tasks and reducing the amount of manual labor required to produce content, AI-driven content creation tools can help you save both time and money.

In the case of businesses, AI can help reduce the need to hire additional content creators or freelancers, thereby lowering overhead costs.

Furthermore, AI-driven content creation tools often come with subscription-based pricing models, making them an affordable option for businesses of all sizes.

For individuals, AI can help reduce the time spent on content creation, allowing them to focus on other tasks or pursue additional income-generating opportunities.

This can be particularly beneficial for freelancers and content creators who need to maximize their time and resources to stay competitive in their respective industries.

- **Enhanced Creativity and Diversity of Ideas:** AI-driven content creation tools can also enhance creativity and promote a diversity of ideas. By analyzing vast amounts of data, AI can identify patterns and trends that may not be immediately apparent to humans, generating fresh ideas and unique perspectives that can help you create more engaging and captivating content.

Additionally, AI can help overcome writer's block by suggesting topics, providing inspiration, and even drafting content based on your input.

This can be particularly helpful for content creators who may struggle with coming up with new ideas or finding the right words to express their thoughts.

By leveraging the creative potential of AI, you can infuse your content with a greater variety of ideas and perspectives, making it more appealing to a wider range of audiences and setting your work apart from the competition.

- **Consistent Quality and Style:** Maintaining consistent quality and style across all content types and platforms can be challenging, especially when juggling multiple content formats and distribution channels. This is where AI-driven content creation tools can offer significant advantages.

AI can help maintain a consistent level of quality across all content types and platforms by adhering to predefined guidelines and templates.

This ensures that your content always meets the desired standards, regardless of the format or distribution channel.

Furthermore, AI can analyze your existing content and learn from it, enabling you to maintain a consistent style and tone across all your work.

By leveraging AI to ensure consistent quality and style, you can build credibility and trust with your audience, fostering stronger relationships and driving long-term engagement with your content.

After selecting the right AI solution for your content creation needs, it is crucial to adapt the tool to your brand voice and style.

This ensures consistency across all content generated by the AI and reinforces your brand identity.

To adapt the AI tool to your brand voice and style, follow these steps to create a priming text block similar to the one used in the previous chapter.

The priming document should contain text relating to the following elements:

- **Examples of writing for voice and style.**
  Pick your best ads, landing pages and blog posts or social media content, paying special attention to include anything that converted well, got a lot of conversations going, or went viral.
- **Glossary of terms**.
  Any language that is not dictionary definable such as brand names, product lines or any technical jargon that will be used frequently should be included.
- **Product benefits and features.**
  Any lists of technical specifications, comparisons to the competition, FAQ or reviews that you would share with a human freelancer or staff writer should be included.

As in previous examples, the master priming prompt should include all the relevant background and context, as well as the AIPS roles that you want the AI to "play".

The format (article, social posts, etc.) and the context, tone and topic can all be added later during your content generation conversation with the AIPS writers you assign to help you.

A generic boardroom prompt is the best place to start I find.

Pretty much every late-night TV show you ever watched had a team of writers all working, debating and collaborating to come up with fresh and relevant content for each show.

This model is a good one for just about any content generation challenge as it will give you a bunch of different viewpoints and ideas from which to choose as you develop the content for publication.

The Writing Team Generic Priming Prompt

"Please create me a simulation of a work session with a team of writers. Your role will be play the part of all participants as well as to facilitate the dialog and debate between a team of writing, marketing and copywriting experts. There are at least 6 top performers collaborating in the room, the goal is to generate the best ideas possible for the topic, context, length of the content to be generated, which will be defined later. When the assignment is defined, engage all the collaborators present in a vigorous debate, incorporating each expert's unique perspective, to create a list of the best ideas. Please begin the session by acknowledging the task I have set before you, and ask me to define the assignment, making sure to include topic, length, platform for distribution in the assignment language, and if that is left out, ask me so that you have all the information needed to get great content out of the experts in the meeting. Thank you.

Here are some examples of writing for the team to analyze that have been successful for us in the past.

INSERT PRIMING TEXT BLOCK HERE"

When posted to the AI, your "team" of writers have been created and are ready to be assigned a new writing challenge.

Since we created all the priming text blocks for "80/20 inc." we built in the previous chapter, I fed that data in after the prompt above.

The AI gave me it's acknowledgment statement and is now ready for any assignment.

Let's give it an interesting challenge...

Let's say that you want to distribute a consistent message across a number of different media types and platforms.

I want to show you the power of both the "AIPS" (Artificial Intelligence Personality Simulator" and the mastermind/boardroom/team style of generating ideas and content for your marketing.

So, let's say that we are facing a new month and have absolutely no clue about what to write about.

Well, if this were a human based interaction with a team of writers...

What would you do?

You would ask them to brainstorm a list of relevant topics and ideas for engaging content, right?

So, let's treat this group of AIPS writers we have just spawned exactly the same.

Let's just ask them to do this work for us as if they were real humans all experts at their craft, all being paid a salary!

Brainstorm Session For The Writing Team Prompt

"Please brainstorm and debate and come up with a list of 10 great topics for a content marketing campaign for our 80/20 software. The topics are also headlines and we need them to be engaging so that they pop off the page of the social media platforms and get clicks, views and likes. I'm excited to see what you all come up with, give me your best work for maximum engagement and virality."

This simple assignment prompt works so well because you have already primed the AI with all the relevant context and information it needs to customize the results for your unique circumstances.

The AI delivers the list of topics as asked:

Thank you for providing the assignment. We'll now engage in a brainstorming session to generate 10 engaging headlines for a content marketing campaign for your 80/20 software. Our focus will be on maximizing engagement and virality for the target audience, Fred: The Overworked Business Owner.

1. **Content Writer: "Unlock Hidden Growth Potential: 5 Secrets Your 80/20 Software Will Reveal About Your Business"**
2. **Copywriter: "Supercharge Your Business Growth: How 80/20 Software Unlocks Time and Revenue for Overworked Owners"**
3. **Marketing Expert: "Revolutionize Your Business with Minimal Effort: 80/20 Software's Low-Hanging Fruit Approach"**
4. **Content Writer: "Stop Drowning in Busy Work: Discover**

the 80/20 Software That Will Transform Your Business and Life"

5. Copywriter: "Effortlessly Boost Your Business: Unleash the Power of 80/20 Software for Rapid Growth"

6. Marketing Expert: "From Burnout to Breakthrough: How 80/20 Software Rescues Overworked Business Owners"

7. Content Writer: "Maximize Impact, Minimize Time: The 80/20 Software That's Changing the Game for Small Business Owners"

8. Copywriter: "The Secret Sauce to Accelerated Business Growth: Discover the 80/20 Software Every Owner Needs"

9. Marketing Expert: "Revive Your Stagnant Business: The 80/20 Software That Delivers Results Without Overwhelming You"

10. Content Writer: "Find Your Business Sweet Spot: How 80/20 Software Optimizes Your Strategy for Maximum Success"

The team has generated a list of 10 engaging headlines designed to resonate with your target audience, Fred: The Overworked Business Owner. We aimed for maximum engagement and virality on social media platforms to ensure clicks, views, and likes. Please review the list and let us know if you have any feedback or require any revisions.

If you see anything here you like, then we can take the next step.

Of course, if this isn't what you wanted, you can always tell the AI to rewrite it and change the style, topic, product etc.

Again, the key to being able to direct and assign your AIPS writing team is to think of what language you would use if these were real people in a real team meeting.

Notice how the list shows who "created" the different topics.

If you used specific experts (living or dead) as your AIPS targets, you will be shocked to see how well the AI can simulate their style of work and language choices.

It's truly wild to play with this AIPS concept and get your dream team assembled to help you work on your projects and tasks!

Of all the ideas, I like topic number 7, "Maximize Impact, Minimize Time" the best...Because what business owner wouldn't want to have a bigger impact while working less?

Let's tell our AIPS team to explore that topic and start to generate us some usable content.

Content Generation Request Prompt

"I really like topic 7. Please use that topic and work as a team to create the best possible content marketing pieces for several social platforms. I would like you to create a tweet (emoji's are ok, but no hashtags please), the script for a video that is no longer than 2 minutes (please include storyboard instructions so that the production team can know what visuals to add to the video), and a full length blog post(and let me know what the header image should look like. Then, please write me a prompt for an image generator AI to create this image). The call to action for all content will be to go to 8020.web to learn more about how this software can help their business. Thank you."

The AIPS thinks for a bit and kicks back this reply:

——————————

Thank you for choosing topic 7. We'll work together as a team to create content marketing pieces for various social platforms,

including a tweet, a video script, and a full-length blog post. We'll ensure the call to action directs users to 8020.web to learn more about the software.

———————————

Tweet:

◈ Maximize Impact, Minimize Time! Discover the 80/20 Software that's changing the game for small business owners. Say goodbye to burnout and hello to growth! Visit 8020.web to learn more. ◈

Video Script (2 minutes):

[Storyboard: Text overlay "Maximize Impact, Minimize Time" with an animation of a clock and a growing bar chart]

Narrator: Are you a small business owner struggling to find the time and energy to grow your business?

[Storyboard: Show a stressed business owner at their desk, juggling multiple tasks]

Narrator: Introducing the 80/20 Software, a game-changer for small business owners like you. Our software helps you optimize your strategy, focusing on the most impactful actions while saving you precious time.

[Storyboard: Show the 80/20 Software interface with a user interacting with it]

Narrator: The 80/20 principle states that 80% of your results come from 20% of your efforts. Our software identifies that crucial 20% so you can prioritize tasks and streamline your workload.

[Storyboard: Split screen showing the difference between a chaotic work environment and an organized, efficient one]

Narrator: With our software, you can:

Pinpoint the most effective strategies

Streamline processes and eliminate bottlenecks

Boost revenue while cutting down on stress

[Storyboard: Show a business owner successfully implementing changes and seeing growth in their business]

Narrator: Don't let your business stagnate. Take control and watch it flourish with the help of our 80/20 Software.

[Storyboard: Show the website URL "8020.web" with the call to action]

Narrator: Visit 8020.web today and learn how this revolutionary software can transform your business for the better.

———————

Blog Post:

Title: Maximize Impact, Minimize Time: The 80/20 Software That's Changing the Game for Small Business Owners

[Header Image: An eye-catching image showing a business owner juggling multiple tasks with the 80/20 Software logo and text "Maximize Impact, Minimize Time" prominently displayed]

Intro:

Running a small business is no easy feat. With countless tasks to juggle, it's easy to feel overwhelmed and burned out. But what if there was a way to maximize your impact with minimal time? Introducing the 80/20 Software, a revolutionary tool designed to help small business owners like you streamline your workload and boost your growth.

The 80/20 Principle:

The 80/20 principle, also known as the Pareto principle, states that 80% of your results come from 20% of your efforts. This means that a small number of high-impact actions can produce the majority of your desired outcomes. Our 80/20 Software is designed to help you identify and focus on these crucial tasks.

Key Features and Benefits:

- Identify High-Impact Strategies
- Streamline Processes and Eliminate Bottlenecks
- Boost Revenue and Cut Down on Stress

How It Works:

Our user-friendly software analyzes your business data and identifies the most effective strategies for growth. By focusing on the top 20% of tasks that drive 80% of your results, you can streamline your processes, eliminate bottlenecks, and boost your revenue, all while cutting down on stress and burnout.

Case Study:

[Include a case study of a small business owner who successfully used the 80/20 Software to transform their business]

John, a small business owner like you, was struggling to keep up with the demands of his company. He felt overwhelmed and burnt out, with little time left for his family and personal life. That's when he discovered the 80/20 Software.

By using our software, John was able to pinpoint the most impactful strategies for his business. He streamlined his processes, eliminated bottlenecks, and ultimately boosted his revenue by 30% within just a few months. The best part? He achieved all of this without sacrificing his work-life balance.

So, don't let your business stagnate due to overwhelm and burnout. Maximize your impact and minimize your time investment with the 80/20 Software. It's time to take control of your business and watch it flourish.

If you are ready to revolutionize the way you run your business? Visit 8020.web today to learn more about how our 80/20 Software can help you achieve the growth and success you deserve.

Header Image Prompt for an AI Image Generator:

An image depicting a small business owner juggling multiple tasks, with the 80/20 Software logo and text "Maximize Impact, Minimize Time" displayed prominently. The image should have a modern and professional feel, appealing to small business owners looking for solutions to their challenges.

We hope you find these content marketing pieces suitable for your campaign. Please let us know if you require any revisions or additional content.

I like the tweet and the video script, but the blog seems a bit simple and robotic. Let's ask the "team" to spice things up a bit.

Revising The Blog Post Prompt

"Please rewrite the blog post, so that it is more story based and engaging. Make sure to reinforce the point of the Pareto Principle, that most people waste time, energy and money working on the things

that don't bring the biggest impact into their business. You could also as the case study use the story of our client Jim, who used our software to analyze the impact of his operations and discovered to his shock, that his best conversion, re-order and margin was not coming from his main product, but being generated from an upsell within his sales funnel. He created a new funnel with this upsell as the primary offer and dramatically increased his sales, profits and lowered his cost to acquire a customer. Thank you."

Here is the revised blog post based on the new instructions.

Title: A Tale of Transformation: How the Pareto Principle and 80/20 Software Revitalized a Small Business

[Header Image: A captivating image of a small business owner with a laptop, demonstrating the growth of his business through charts and graphs]

Introduction:

There's a famous principle in business and life called the Pareto Principle, which states that 80% of our results come from just 20% of our efforts. However, many people waste time, energy, and money working on tasks that don't yield the greatest impact. Today, I want to share the remarkable story of our client, Jim, who harnessed the power of the Pareto Principle through our innovative 80/20 Software, transforming his business and reaping the rewards of focusing on high-impact tasks.

Jim, a dedicated small business owner, felt like he was working tirelessly to grow his business, but the results just weren't showing. He knew about the Pareto Principle but struggled to identify which tasks and strategies would provide the most impact for his business.

Upon discovering the 80/20 Software, Jim decided to give it a try. He hoped that by analyzing his operations, he could uncover the high-impact tasks that would propel his business to new heights.

Little did he know, he was in for a shock.

As the software analyzed Jim's business, it revealed that his main product wasn't driving his best conversions, reorders, and profit margins. Instead, these impressive results were coming from an upsell within his sales funnel. Armed with this valuable insight, Jim decided to make a bold move.

Jim created a new sales funnel, placing the upsell as the primary offer. This shift in strategy paid off handsomely. He saw a dramatic increase in sales, profits, and customer satisfaction. Furthermore, his cost to acquire a customer significantly decreased, making his business more efficient and competitive.

Jim's story demonstrates the power of the Pareto Principle and the transformative potential of the 80/20 Software. By focusing on the high-impact tasks that drive the majority of results, small business owners can streamline their operations, boost profits, and enjoy a better work-life balance.

If you're ready to unlock the hidden potential of your business, visit 8020.web today to learn more about how our 80/20 Software can help you uncover the most impactful tasks and strategies for your success.

If this revised version is acceptable, then you can add any finishing touches and publish it.

If it's too short, just ask your "team" of AIPS writers to expand it.

If you want to have them expand one section, idea, add a concept, just ask!

As you begin to experiment and explore the possibilities for revision and guiding the writing process, you will realize that unlike in the past, where getting one version was so tough, now you can literally have your team write the story 10 different ways and you can choose one or assemble the best bits from all 10 as you choose!

Are you starting to see why, in the beginning of this book I introduced you to the "bottega model" as an optimal way to interact with AI?

It's a perfect metaphor for the workflow you have just seen presented which produces the best results with consistency.

Did the team of AIPS writers create the perfect content?

NO!

But it was pretty darn good, and so now you or one of your human team as the "Master" can put the finishing touches to make it truly special.

As somebody who has written two books "the hard way", (***Mastering Futures Trading*** and ***Optimize Your Trading Edge***) I know that the most difficult and most time consuming part for me was the outline, planning, story arc, etc.

Once I had that basic structure built, I could very easily find the words to fill out the concepts I wanted to share with my readers.

Because of how easy it is to have AI give you a bunch of options to choose from, you can almost always spark your creative juices and get past the hardest part of "writer's block"...A blank page.

By building the primer text blocks and the AIPS dream team, you are in a position to paste in this series of prompts and text blocks in a matter of moments to "spawn" a new team and a new work session.

Due to the state of the technology as I write this, the memory for remembering past conversations is limited, so it is a best practice to start a new session and prime the AIPS team using the process shown above, each time you want to generate a new assignment.

If you leave a session open and go into a long series of work sessions, you may notice that the AIPS models drift and revert to a more canned and robotic default set of language styles as your initial definition of your mix of experts gets "forgotten" and the AI reverts back to the basics.

If you experience this "drift", simply start a new session and prime the AIPS models so that they have all your information and context "fresh" in their memories.

This issue will likely be fixed soon, so by the time you read this, likely this will not be an issue...but I wanted to include it because it can cause confusion and frustration when using the versions of AI that are currently available.

Chapter 6
The AI Sales Machine:
Dominate Lead Generation and
Crush Your Competition

In the past, sales and lead generation techniques were predominantly manual, time-consuming, and labor-intensive.

Sales teams relied on cold calling, door-to-door sales, and direct mail campaigns to reach potential customers.

These traditional methods were often hit-or-miss, with low conversion rates and high costs associated with maintaining a large sales force.

With the advent of the internet and digital marketing, sales and lead generation techniques have evolved considerably.

Businesses now have access to a wide array of online channels, such as email marketing, social media advertising, search engine optimization (SEO), and content marketing, to reach their target audience.

The use of data analytics and customer relationship management (CRM) systems has also enabled organizations to track and analyze customer interactions, improving the efficiency and effectiveness of their sales and lead generation efforts.

Before you can begin crafting effective prompts for AI-driven sales and lead generation, it is essential to have a clear understanding of your sales goals and target audience.

This will enable you to create prompts that resonate with your ideal customers and drive them towards the desired action.

Let's regenerate the AIPS writing team using the prompt shared in the previous chapter, except instead of AIPS "writers" we will change the language to "marketers and salespeople" in the first sentence...

The Marketing and Sales Team Generic Priming Prompt

"Please create me a simulation of a work session with a team of top marketers and high performance salespeople. Your role will be play the part of all participants as well as to facilitate the dialog and debate between a team of writing, marketing and copywriting experts. There are at least 6 top performers collaborating in the room, the goal is to generate the best ideas possible for the topic, context, length of the content to be generated, which will be defined later. When the assignment is defined, engage all the collaborators present in a vigorous debate, incorporating each expert's unique perspective, to create a list of the best ideas. Please begin the session by acknowledging the task I have set before you, and ask me to define the assignment, making sure to include topic, length, platform for distribution in the assignment language, and if that is left out, ask me so that you have all the information needed to get great content out of the experts in the meeting. Thank you.

Here are some examples of writing for the team to analyze that have been successful for us in the past.

INSERT PRIMING TEXT BLOCK HERE"

Now, with our AIPS team ready, let's put them to work.

Let's focus them on lead generation with the following prompt:

Lead Generator Brainstorming Prompt

"Please begin a brainstorming session on how to generate leads for our 80/20 software. Our control lead generator page converts at 12% and the goal of this session is to think of highly creative and off the wall ideas to beat that control. Please think outside the box and vigorously debate and poke holes in the ideas that are shared so that I can clearly understand each participant's thought process. The output of this brainstorming session should be for a web-based landing page, with cold traffic driven to it from paid ads on social media. Thank you."

The AI takes this input and begins the brainstorming process:

Team, let's begin our brainstorming session on how to generate leads for our 80/20 software with the goal of beating the current 12% conversion rate on our control lead generator page. We're looking for highly creative and out-of-the-box ideas that can be incorporated into a web-based landing page with cold traffic driven from paid ads on social media. Remember, we want to vigorously debate and poke holes in the ideas presented to ensure that we understand each participant's thought process. Let's get started!

Sarah (Digital Marketing Expert): How about using interactive content, such as a quiz or assessment, that helps the user identify areas where they could benefit from the 80/20 software? This would engage the user, provide value, and ultimately lead them to see the software as a solution to their problem.

David (Sales Strategy Expert): I like the idea of using interactive content, but I worry that a quiz might not be specific enough to showcase the unique features of our software. What if we used a calculator that allows users to input their business data and see the potential impact of adopting the 80/20 approach?

Ava (Copywriting Expert): I agree with David that the calculator idea could be more effective than a quiz. However, we need to ensure that the copy on the landing page conveys a sense of urgency and exclusivity. What if we offer a limited-time discount or bonus for users who complete the calculator and sign up for the software?

James (Content Marketing Expert): I like the idea of a limited-time offer, but I think we could also explore some unconventional marketing tactics to capture attention. For example, what if we created an engaging video that tells a compelling story of a struggling business owner who transformed their business using the 80/20 software? This could be a powerful way to connect with our target audience on an emotional level.

Liam (SEO Expert): While I think the video is a great idea, we need to make sure that the landing page is also optimized for SEO. This could involve strategically placing target keywords throughout the copy and ensuring that the meta tags are optimized to drive organic traffic.

Sophia (UX/UI Designer): I understand the importance of SEO, but we also need to ensure that the landing page has a clean and intuitive design. A strong visual hierarchy and clear call-to-action are crucial for guiding users through the page and encouraging them to take action.

Sarah (Digital Marketing Expert): I believe the interactive content, such as the calculator, is a good idea. But we should also consider utilizing retargeting ads for those who interact with the calculator but don't sign up. This could help us reach out to potential customers who may need a gentle reminder or a stronger incentive to sign up.

David (Sales Strategy Expert): I agree with Sarah on retargeting ads, but I think we should also consider using customer testimonials or case studies, like Jim's story, on the landing page. This will add credibility and trust to our software, which could potentially increase conversion rates.

Ava (Copywriting Expert): While testimonials and case studies are valuable, I think we should also focus on crafting a compelling headline that captures the essence of the 80/20 software. This will help grab users' attention and entice them to explore the landing page further.

James (Content Marketing Expert): I still believe in the power of storytelling, especially through video. We could also create a series of blog posts and social media content that expands on the stories of successful users of our software. This will help potential customers understand the real-life benefits of using our product.

Liam (SEO Expert): While content creation is important, I think we should also consider optimizing the landing page for voice search. As voice search becomes more popular, ensuring that our landing page is easily discoverable through voice queries will be crucial for driving traffic.

Sophia (UX/UI Designer): I think it's important to strike a balance between creative content and a user-friendly design. We could use A/B testing to determine which design elements and content pieces perform best, allowing us to optimize the landing page for maximum conversions.

After the debate, the team can now synthesize these ideas to create a multi-faceted approach for the landing page. This could include incorporating interactive content like a calculator, crafting a compelling headline, optimizing for SEO and voice search, using retargeting ads, and leveraging storytelling through video and customer testimonials. By blending these strategies and testing different design elements and content pieces, the team can work towards creating a landing page that surpasses the current 12% conversion rate.

Notice how each expert engages in the debate with a bias for their area of expertise? Hopefully this debate gives some good ideas. If not, we can ask the team directly to make us a list based on the discussion to this point.

Create List Of Lead Generation Ideas Prompt

"Please make me a list of 5 lead generation topics based on your debate and all your experience in your field. Please talk about each one and pick only the top ten that have the most support from the team members. Thank you."

The AI team comes back with this response:

- **Free Assessment or Audit: Offer a free business assessment or audit that identifies areas for improvement and growth. This idea has strong support from the team as it demonstrates the value our software can bring to the customer's business.**
- **Webinar or Online Workshop: Host a webinar or online workshop on effective business growth strategies, incorporating our software as a solution. The team believes that providing valuable educational content can attract leads and showcase the software's benefits.**
- **eBook or Whitepaper: Create an eBook or whitepaper on the 80/20 principle and how it applies to business growth. The team supports this idea because it positions our company as an expert in the field and encourages potential**

customers to share their contact information in exchange for valuable content.

- **Email Course:** Develop a free email course that educates potential customers on the Pareto Principle and its applications in business growth. The team agrees that an email course can create trust and demonstrate expertise, leading to more leads.
- **Social Media Giveaway:** Organize a social media giveaway contest where participants can win a free subscription to our software. The team supports this idea as it can generate buzz around our product and attract more leads through social sharing.

These top five lead generation ideas, backed by the team members, cover a wide range of strategies, including content creation, events, social media, collaborations, and promotions. By implementing these ideas, the team aims to attract and convert more leads for our 80/20 software.

Let's use our AIPS team to outline and script a 30 minute webinar and see if that can outperform our control which is a free trial.

Since not all those who get a free trial engage with the software to see how good it is, there is an opportunity here.

If the webinar is compelling, perhaps we can just sell the software without the trial period and increase sales while also only paying onboarding and support costs for those who have indicated that they want the value the software provides since they were willing to pay for it!

Webinar Outline Development Prompt

"Please put all your expertise together and create an outline for a 30 minute webinar to sell our 80/20 software which helps the user define what business segments and actions give them the biggest impact on their bottom line due to the Pareto principle. This webinar should start with a hook segment of about 3 minutes that engages and excites the audience enough that they stay tuned and listen to the entire presentation. Next, use stories and use case examples to make the case that most businesses don't know where their biggest money makers truly are, because they never did a data driven analysis guided by the 80/20 rule principles. Then make an offer that they can get access to this software for 6 months for a lump sum of $58 that's equal to 2 months access at the regular price. After this promotional 6 month period is done, their subscription would revert to our standard monthly rate of $29 per month. Use all the best practices of selling and closing to make this an irresistible offer. Thank you."

The AI team comes back with the following outline:

Title: Discover the Hidden Goldmine in Your Business: Unlock the Power of the 80/20 Principle with Our Revolutionary Software

Webinar Outline:

I. Introduction and Hook (3 minutes)

A. Start with a surprising statistic or statement that grabs attention

B. Share a relatable story of a struggling business owner

C. Introduce the 80/20 Principle and its potential impact on their business

II. The Problem: Most Businesses Don't Know Their Biggest Moneymakers (7 minutes)

A. Explain the common pitfalls and misconceptions in identifying high-impact actions

B. Discuss the importance of data-driven analysis for business growth

C. Share real-life examples of businesses that were unaware of their most profitable segments

III. The Solution: Our 80/20 Software (10 minutes)

A. Introduce the software and its features

B. Explain how it utilizes the Pareto Principle to identify high-impact actions

C. Present case studies of businesses that transformed their growth using our software

D. Demonstrate the software with a live walkthrough

IV. The Offer: Exclusive 6-Month Access for Just $58 (5 minutes)

A. Present the limited-time offer of 6 months access for the price of 2 months

B. Emphasize the savings and benefits, including reverting to the standard rate after the promotional period

C. Share testimonials from satisfied customers who have taken advantage of the offer

V. Addressing Objections and Frequently Asked Questions (3 minutes)

A. Address common concerns, such as time commitment, technical expertise, and effectiveness

B. Provide clear, concise answers to anticipated questions

VI. Closing and Call to Action (2 minutes)

A. Recap the benefits of the software and the exclusive offer

B. Create a sense of urgency by emphasizing the limited availability of the offer

C. Encourage attendees to visit 8020.web to learn more and sign up for the promotional offer

This outline incorporates a compelling hook, addresses the problem businesses face, showcases the solution, presents an irresistible offer, addresses objections, and closes with a strong call to action. By following these steps, the webinar aims to generate interest and drive sales of the 80/20 software.

Now, you can ask for any changes or revisions you might like to experiment with.

Once you have an outline that you like, it's better to ask the AIPS team to create the script in chunks.

Since this book is designed to teach you process and how to structure your prompts, let's not waste energy creating made up features and benefits for our made up 80/20 software.

Instead, let's ask the AIPS team to script out just one section and from that interaction you will have the knowledge you need to reproduce this process for your unique product or service.

Script Out A Section Of The Outline Prompt

"Please write me the script for the following section of the outline. As indicated, the script should be able to be presented within a 7 minute time limitation. Thank you.

II. The Problem: Most Businesses Don't Know Their Biggest Moneymakers (7 minutes)

A. Explain the common pitfalls and misconceptions in identifying high-impact actions

B. Discuss the importance of data-driven analysis for business growth

C. Share real-life examples of businesses that were unaware of their most profitable segments"

The AIPS team responds to this request with the following script:

[Slide 1: The Problem]

Host: Now, let's dive into the problem that plagues so many businesses. Most business owners simply don't know where their biggest moneymakers are hiding. This is due to a few common pitfalls and misconceptions when it comes to identifying high-impact actions.

[Slide 2: Common Pitfalls and Misconceptions]

Host: The first pitfall is that business owners often focus on what they're most comfortable

with, rather than what's most effective. They may pour time and resources into tasks they enjoy or feel competent in, even if those tasks don't have the highest impact on their bottom line.

Secondly, many businesses fail to analyze their data effectively. They might track their sales or other metrics, but they don't dig deep enough to uncover the hidden patterns and trends that reveal their most profitable actions and segments.

[Slide 3: Importance of Data-Driven Analysis]

Host: This brings us to the importance of data-driven analysis for business growth. With the right tools and mindset, you can uncover valuable insights from your data, allowing you to make informed decisions about where to focus your time, energy, and resources. By concentrating on the areas with the most significant impact, you can accelerate your business growth and achieve your goals faster.

[Slide 4: Real-Life Example 1 – Jim's Surprising Discovery]

Host: Let me share a story that illustrates this point. Meet Jim, a business owner who thought his main product was the primary driver of his revenue. After using our 80/20 software to analyze his operations, he was shocked to discover that his best conversion, re-order, and margin were actually coming from an upsell within his sales funnel.

[Slide 5: Real-Life Example 2 – The Boutique's Hidden Gem]

Host: Another example is a boutique clothing store that thought their best-selling items were their trendiest clothes. After analyzing their sales data, they realized that a particular line of high-quality basics was responsible for the majority of their profits. By refocusing their marketing efforts and inventory on these basics, they saw a dramatic increase in sales and profits.

[Slide 6: Real-Life Example 3 – The Restaurant's Secret Ingredient]

Host: Lastly, let's look at a restaurant that believed their main attraction was their extensive menu. After analyzing customer feedback and sales data, they found out that a few signature dishes were driving the majority of their revenue. By streamlining their menu and highlighting these dishes, they were able to reduce costs, improve customer satisfaction, and increase profits.

[Slide 7: Recap]

Host: These examples show that many businesses are unaware of their most profitable segments. They illustrate the importance of data-driven analysis in identifying high-impact actions and strategies. By focusing on what truly drives your business, you can maximize your growth potential and unlock hidden opportunities.

Our 80/20 software is designed to help businesses like yours analyze and pinpoint the areas that bring the most significant impact to your bottom line. By leveraging the power of the Pareto Principle, our software can help you identify the 20% of your efforts that generate 80% of your results. With this invaluable insight, you can strategically focus your time, energy, and resources on the most crucial aspects of your business, maximizing growth and profitability. Don't let hidden opportunities slip through the cracks. Harness the power of 80/20 software today and unlock your business's true potential.

Does the case study about Jim sound familiar?

Isn't it exciting how the AI remembers your previous work and includes that relevant story into the webinar script?

Assuming you like this language and don't have revisions, you are now ready to recycle the simple prompt above to generate the script for the next section in the presentation.

But before we move on, what if you want help with the slides?

Let's ask the team to give us some guidance there...

Slide Description Generation Prompt

"This script is great, thanks. Now, before we go to the next section, can you give me a detailed description of what should be on each slide for this section of the presentation that you just scripted for me. Please be detailed about formatting and style, setup etc. If an image is appropriate, write for me the exact language of a prompt for an image generation AI so that I can copy and paste that in to create the exact image needed. Thank you."

Boom!

Here is your list of slides to be made, offering clear guidance as well as basic prompts for image generation to give to whoever (or whatever AI) you will have build your images for your slide deck for you!

Slide 1:

Title: The Problem

Subtitle: Uncovering Your Biggest Moneymakers

Formatting: Bold title, subtitle in italics

Background: Simple, clean, light-colored background

Slide 2:

Title: Common Pitfalls and Misconceptions

Bullets:

- **Focusing on comfort rather than effectiveness**
- **Inadequate data analysis**

Formatting: Bold title, bullet points for each pitfall

Background: Simple, clean, light-colored background

Image prompt: "Create an image of a business owner looking confused, surrounded by papers and charts, symbolizing the struggle to find their biggest moneymakers."

Slide 3:

Title: Importance of Data-Driven Analysis

Bullets:

- Uncovering valuable insights
- Making informed decisions
- Accelerating business growth

Formatting: Bold title, bullet points for each benefit

Background: Simple, clean, light-colored background

Image prompt: "Create an image of a magnifying glass over a bar chart, symbolizing the detailed analysis needed to uncover hidden business insights."

Slide 4:

Title: Real-Life Example 1 – Jim's Surprising Discovery

Subtitle: Upsell within Sales Funnel

Formatting: Bold title, subtitle in italics

Background: Simple, clean, light-colored background

Image prompt: "Create an image of a surprised businessman looking at a laptop displaying a sales funnel, symbolizing Jim's discovery of the profitable upsell."

Slide 5:

Title: Real-Life Example 2 – The Boutique's Hidden Gem

Subtitle: High-Quality Basics

Formatting: Bold title, subtitle in italics

Background: Simple, clean, light-colored background

Image prompt: "Create an image of a clothing rack with high-quality basic garments, symbolizing the boutique's hidden source of profit."

Slide 6:

Title: Real-Life Example 3 – The Restaurant's Secret Ingredient

Subtitle: Signature Dishes

Formatting: Bold title, subtitle in italics

Background: Simple, clean, light-colored background

Image prompt: "Create an image of a restaurant menu highlighting a few signature dishes, symbolizing the discovery of the true revenue drivers."

Slide 7:

Title: Recap

Subtitle: The Power of Data-Driven Analysis

Bullets:

- Identifying high-impact actions

- Maximizing growth potential
- Unlocking hidden opportunities

Formatting: Bold title, subtitle in italics, bullet points for each recap point

Background: Simple, clean, light-colored background

Image prompt: "Create an image of a key unlocking a treasure chest, symbolizing the hidden opportunities uncovered through data-driven analysis."

As always, you can use this AI generated content as it comes out or ask for any revisions you wish.

Once you are satisfied with the output, edit and adjust to make a finished product that you will be proud to use in front of an audience of prospective buyers.

Once you have generated all your scripting elements, you may have filled up the AI's memory, so a reminder of the outline would be prudent if you want the AIPS marketing team to help you write your ads for the webinar.

Paid Ad Generation Prompt

"Please write me three ads based on the outline we have created together. One ad should be optimized for Facebook, one for LinkedIn and one for Twitter. The goal of these ads should be to capture the attention of a cold prospect so that they stop scrolling and feel like they must register for this webinar to get the information it promises. Ask them to click on the link below to register for this event and discover how much money you may be leaving on the table. I will paste the outline below as a reminder. Thank you!

OUTLINE PASTED HERE"

And as fast as you can get a drink of water while you wait, your ads are ready for your approval!

If you want another version of each ad for A/B testing purposes, that's also easy and fast to request...

A/B Testing Version Prompt

"Please rewrite all three ads with some variations for A/B testing purposes, and make these versions extra creative and compelling! Thank you."

And there you have it, a second set of ads for testing and comparison purposes!

Facebook Ad (Variation B):

◇Unleash Your Business's Hidden Potential!◇

Frustrated with slow growth? The secret to success might be right in front of you. Discover the power of the 80/20 principle in our must-attend webinar and unlock the high-impact actions that can transform your business.

◇Register now and stop missing out on the profits you deserve!◇

[Link to Webinar Registration]

LinkedIn Ad (Variation B):

Revolutionize Your Business with the 80/20 Principle

Attention ambitious business owners! Tired of strategies that fail to deliver real results? Our exclusive webinar reveals the

game-changing 80/20 principle that can help you focus on the actions that really matter.

Don't let this opportunity pass you by. Register now and uncover the hidden profits in your business!

[Link to Webinar Registration]

Twitter Ad (Variation B):

◈**Supercharge your business with the 80/20 rule! Discover the secret to skyrocketing success in our exclusive webinar. Time to claim the profits you've been missing! Register here**◈

[Link to Webinar Registration]

With the examples shared in this chapter, you can see how much faster you can plan, organize, generate and revise the content you need for any lead generation task.

Need emails for follow up or prospecting?

Just ask...

All the priming that has been done to give the AIPS team the context it needs to generate quality, customized content is there in its memory bank to refer to as it accomplishes its assignments you give it.

As the memory, sophistication and speed of these systems continue to grow, the priming process will become less cumbersome, repetitive and simplistic.

Soon there will be an opportunity to share all the work you and your team generate with grades and real world results to share with the AI as it learns more and more about the patterns and processes that work best for your unique needs.

But, back to the core theme of this book...

No matter how many flights of fancy I go down about future technological possibilities, I can't see a future that doesn't use carefully crafted natural language-based prompts as the core user interface for the systems we interact with.

Being able to craft the exact language "programs" to instruct these systems what to do and how to do it will remain a critical skill, and one that separates those who succeed at the highest levels and those who work for those who have these prompt engineering skills.

Chapter 7
Market Research Reimagined:
Uncover Hidden Treasures with AI's Unparalleled Wisdom

Market research is a crucial component of any business strategy, as it helps organizations understand their target audience, competitors, and industry trends. It enables businesses to make data informed decisions, identify new opportunities, and develop products and services that cater to the needs and preferences of their customers.

Traditionally, market research has relied on costly, labor-intensive and time-consuming methods, such as surveys, focus groups, and interviews.

While these techniques can yield valuable insights, they are often costly and may not provide a comprehensive understanding of the market landscape.

Moreover, the rapidly changing business environment and the emergence of digital channels have led to an explosion of data, making it increasingly challenging for businesses to analyze and derive actionable insights from the information.

The advent of artificial intelligence (AI) has brought about a transformation in the field of market research, enabling businesses to harness the power of data to unlock new possibilities.

AI-driven market research techniques are revolutionizing the industry by offering faster, more accurate, and cost-effective solutions.

The following are some key ways in which AI is reshaping market research:

- **Automated data collection and analysis:** AI-powered tools can automatically collect and analyze vast amounts of data from various sources, such as social media, online forums, and customer reviews. These tools can process unstructured data, such as text, images, and videos, enabling businesses to gain a deeper understanding of their target audience's preferences, needs, and behaviors. Additionally, AI-driven analytics can identify patterns and trends in the data, providing businesses with actionable insights that inform their strategies.

- **Sentiment analysis:** Sentiment analysis, also known as opinion mining, uses AI to determine the emotions and opinions expressed in textual data, such as social media posts, online reviews, and blog comments. By analyzing the sentiment of consumers towards a brand, product, or service, businesses can gauge customer satisfaction, identify areas for improvement, and track the effectiveness of marketing campaigns.

- **Predictive analytics:** AI-driven predictive analytics leverages machine learning algorithms to analyze historical data and predict future outcomes, such as customer behavior, market trends, and sales performance. This enables businesses to make proactive decisions, anticipate market shifts, and capitalize on emerging opportunities.

- **Competitive intelligence:** AI-powered tools can monitor and analyze competitors' activities, such as product launches, marketing campaigns, and pricing strategies. This information enables businesses to stay ahead of the competition, identify potential threats, and uncover new opportunities.

Let's work through some of these concepts and engineer some prompts to accomplish "AI Collaborative Acceleration Magic" together.

For many with an idea and a dream of starting a business, the actual "getting started" is the hardest part.

AI can assist in this process by helping you identify the people who are most likely to buy your product, and help you define all the steps you need to take in order to turn your dream into a reality in the business world.

Let's pretend that we are at the very beginning or the business development process.

For this thought experiment, we are currently employed, but in a job that doesn't pay enough and is very boring to us.

We have time in the evenings and weekends to devote to building a second income, with the hopes that it will eventually pay well enough to allow us to quit the job we are so bored with so we can focus on growing this business and expanding our income.

We want to develop a product that we can sell through the many E-commerce platforms, which will take care of all the billing, shipping and fulfillment.

The perfect product would be something that we can have manufactured and shipped directly to the platform's fulfillment centers, so our only tasks would be customer support, marketing and promotion and new product development.

We just want a better life and don't have a great idea yet, so where do we start?

This is the horrifying "facing a brick wall" experience many writers describe where they are faced with a blank page and a blank mind.

We all know the saying…"The journey of 1,000 miles starts with a single step".

But…

What is that step?

Well, if you have an AI assistant to help you, AI has a vast store of information from which to draw from to help guide you to profitable inspirations.

As with any prompt, we must be clear on our goal and what we want the AI to produce.

So with that in mind, let's begin the process…

Unique Product AIPS Design Team Prompt

"Please make a large list of the best designers, toymakers, scientists and engineers ever assembled. These people have created and brought many successful products to market. Their products often go viral and become the fad gift or toy of that season. They understand what makes a product unique and how to design it so that it jumps off the page on social media and makes the reader say "wow, I WANT THAT!". They also have an expert understanding of price points and manufacturing costs, so that they can come up with ideas that are practical and jaw droppingly innovative, yet simple enough to be inexpensive to manufacture so that they provide great profit margins. It is critical that you have enough information about each person to accurately simulate their experience and wisdom, so do not include any for

whom you have a limited dataset. You will play the role of all these simulated people internally and also the role of the facilitator and only you will directly interact with me. Once you have my input, please go back to the group of people you have assembled and have a vigorous brainstorming and creative debate session, then report back to me the best ideas and solutions that the group can come up with. Thank you."

This is another generic primer style prompt.

It does not produce any specific output, but it sets up the scenario you want the AI to play with so that you can ask it any question and get a much better answer than a simple search query type prompt.

To ram this lesson home, let's just compare the outputs to the same question when an AI is primed from the richly worded prompt above, compared to when you just ask the question alone...

If I ask the AI in a new session without any context or primer prompt to:

"Please tell me the top 5 market segments where products that are $100 or less tend to consistently go viral on social media?"

An unprimed AI session returns the following output:

- **Beauty and Skincare Products: Cosmetics and skincare products have consistently been popular items that go viral on social media. Products that offer unique features or innovative packaging have the potential to catch the attention of social media users.**

- **Fashion Accessories: Jewelry, hats, scarves, and other fashion accessories are another market segment that has seen products go viral on social media. The key is to offer** products that are trendy, stylish, and affordable.

-

- **Health and Wellness Products:** Health and wellness products, such as fitness equipment, supplements, and essential oils, have gained popularity on social media platforms due to the increasing interest in self-care and wellness.

- **Home Decor and Gadgets:** Home decor and gadgets, such as LED lights, smart home devices, and decorative items, have also seen products go viral on social media. The key is to offer products that are unique and offer value for the price.

- **Pet Products:** Pet products, such as toys, grooming supplies, and accessories, have also gained popularity on social media platforms. Products that offer unique features or solve common problems have the potential to go viral among pet owners.

Now, compare the output from the exact same question when we ask a "pre-primed" AI that has been properly primed by using the "Unique Product AIPS Design Team Prompt" posted above.

After simulating the brainstorming and creative debate session with the assembled experts, we have identified the top 5 market segments where products that are $100 or less tend to consistently go viral on social media:

- **Tech Gadgets & Accessories:** Inexpensive technology gadgets and accessories, such as smartphone cases, wireless earbuds, smartphone camera lenses, portable chargers, and smart home devices, often become popular due to their utility and novelty. These products appeal to a wide range of consumers and can quickly gain traction on social media platforms as users share their experiences and reviews.

- Personal Care & Beauty: Affordable personal care and beauty products, such as skincare devices, makeup, hair care tools, and wellness items, often go viral due to their promise of self-improvement and their visual appeal. Social media influencers and user-generated content drive the popularity of these products, as people share their routines, results, and product recommendations.

- Toys & Games: Inexpensive toys and games, especially those that cater to nostalgia, challenge the user, or promote creativity, can rapidly gain popularity on social media. Examples include fidget toys, board games, building sets, and educational STEM toys. These products often go viral due to their playfulness and ability to bring people together.

- Fitness & Health: Affordable fitness and health products, such as exercise equipment, wearable devices, and wellness apps, often go viral as they cater to the growing interest in personal health and well-being. Social media challenges, user testimonials, and influencers contribute to the virality of these products, inspiring others to join in and pursue a healthier lifestyle.

- DIY Kits & Hobbies: Do-it-yourself kits and hobby products, like craft kits, model kits, and gardening supplies, can quickly gain traction on social media, as people share their creations and the process of making them. These products appeal to consumers who enjoy hands-on activities and want to learn new skills, and they often gain popularity through online communities, tutorials, and challenges.

These market segments consistently see viral products priced at $100 or less, as they offer novelty, utility, and entertainment value while catering to a wide range of interests and demographics. Social media plays a significant role in driving the popularity of these products, with influencers, user-generated content, and online communities fueling their rapid spread.

If you had paid two different humans to accomplish this task for you, and this was the work product they turned in to you…How would you feel about the difference in the depth and quality of the two lists?

This "in your face" example is why you hear from some people that AI "doesn't work" or "can't produce anything of value".

It's not because the tool is incapable, it's that the quality of the work product you get from the AI, is directly related to the quality of the correctly engineered and tested/optimized prompt that was used to set the AI's assignment!

So let's get back to our product development task.

DIY and hobbies and tech sound fun, but imagine all the expense and development costs to create a new camera lens or earbud?

Hobbies can transform very inexpensive and easy to get items and turn them into something special and valuable. Let's explore this market segment a bit deeper by asking the following question to our primed AI session…

"What are the top 5 communities or subsets of the DIY kits-and hobby market segment that have the biggest number of enthusiasts and ever more important, folks who are enthusiastic buyers in their specific hobby or DIY kits interest?"

The primed AI again responds with a robust and information dense answer...

After further analysis and discussion with the simulated experts, we have identified the top 5 communities or subsets within the DIY and hobby market segment that have the largest number of enthusiasts and, importantly, enthusiastic buyers in their specific hobby or DIY interest:

- **Home Improvement & Woodworking:** This community includes enthusiasts who engage in various home improvement projects, woodworking, and furniture making. These DIYers invest in tools, materials, and instructional resources to enhance their skills and complete their projects. They often share their progress and finished works on social media platforms and forums, driving interest and purchases within this subset.

- **Arts & Crafts:** This broad category encompasses various creative hobbies such as painting, drawing, knitting, crochet, sewing, and jewelry-making. Enthusiastic buyers in this community are passionate about acquiring supplies, tools, and learning resources to improve their craft. Online tutorials, social media influencers, and dedicated platforms for sharing and selling handmade items contribute to the popularity and growth of this market segment.

- Gardening & Urban Farming: Gardening and urban farming enthusiasts focus on cultivating plants, flowers, and food in their homes, yards, or community spaces. These individuals invest in seeds, plants, tools, and other supplies to support their gardening efforts. This community's growth is driven by an increasing interest in sustainability, local food production, and the therapeutic benefits of gardening.

- Electronic Projects & Robotics: This subset consists of individuals interested in building electronic devices, programming, and robotics. They invest in components, microcontrollers, sensors, and other materials to create various electronic projects. This community is fueled by an interest in technology, innovation, and the desire to learn new skills. Online forums, tutorials, and maker spaces contribute to the popularity and growth of this market segment.

- Scale Modeling & Miniatures: Enthusiasts in this community enjoy building and collecting scale models, miniatures, and dioramas, representing various subjects such as vehicles, aircraft, buildings, and scenes from popular culture. These hobbyists invest in kits, tools, paints, and other supplies to create and customize their models. Online forums, social media groups, and events contribute to the community's growth and drive interest in the market segment.

These communities within the DIY and hobby market segment have a significant number of passionate enthusiasts who are eager to invest in their interests, driving demand for products and resources that cater to their specific needs and preferences.

Hmm, we like gardening and crafts, but it seems like crafting fads come and go, and we could get stuck with a lot of building effort for a business with short term lifespan.

On the other hand, plants, flowers and gardens are always pretty much the same in terms of popularity and size of market.

We also know that there are a lot more people who have houseplants vs outdoor gardens.

Some of these would definitely struggle with keeping their houseplants healthy so would be likely willing to pay for a product that would help them keep their plants in tip top shape.

Let's dig deeper into this market segment...

"What are 5 constant problems or irritations that people who love indoor houseplants, flowers, and even cut flower arrangements deal with on a continuous basis, that have easy solutions that nobody knows about and are bad enough problems that they would be willing to pay for a solution to?"

And just like that, the AI spits out some ideas that are actually quite intriguing and perhaps worth pursuing!

After further discussion with the simulated experts, we have identified the top 5 constant problems or irritations that indoor houseplant, flower, and cut flower arrangement enthusiasts face, which have relatively easy solutions that are not widely known and are significant enough for people to be willing to pay for:

- **Root rot prevention: Root rot is a common issue for indoor plants, typically caused by over-watering or poorly draining soil. An easy solution that's not widely known is using a mix of well-draining soil and adding perlite or** pumice to improve aeration. A pre-packaged soil blend specifically designed to prevent root rot could be a product that enthusiasts would be willing to pay for.

-

- **Improving humidity levels:** Many indoor plants require higher humidity levels than typically found in homes, especially during winter months when indoor heating can dry the air. A simple solution is to use a pebble tray filled with water placed under the plant pot, which increases humidity around the plant as the water evaporates. A stylish and functional pebble tray designed specifically for this purpose could be a desirable product.

- **Supporting climbing plants:** Climbing and vining houseplants often need support to grow properly, and enthusiasts may struggle with finding suitable structures. A modular, easy-to-install, and adjustable plant support system that can be adapted for various indoor plants could provide an innovative solution that plant lovers would be willing to pay for.

- **Prolonging the life of cut flower arrangements:** Cut flowers tend to wilt and lose their appeal quickly, which can be frustrating for enthusiasts who enjoy having fresh arrangements in their homes. An easy solution could involve providing plant food sachets or a specialized flower preservation spray to extend the life of cut flowers. A product like this, if not widely known, could generate interest and willingness to purchase.

- **Managing plant clutter and organization:** Indoor plant enthusiasts with numerous plants may struggle with organizing and displaying their collection in an attractive and space-efficient manner. A modular, customizable plant shelving system that can be easily adjusted to accommodate various plant sizes and arrangements could be a sought-after solution.

These are five issues faced by indoor houseplant, flower, and cut flower arrangement enthusiasts that have relatively easy solutions but may not be widely known. Developing and marketing products or services to address these problems could attract a sizable customer base within this niche market.

The cut flower solution is interesting...who doesn't want your flower arrangements to last longer? Also, cut flower arrangements will likely be something that remain available and that people like to buy for many years into the future.

Let's explore this and see if this is something that people think is valuable and might be willing to pay for since we all know there is that packet of plant food that usually comes with every flower arrangement...

"Can you do a virtual set of surveys and focus groups and give me a report on what the cut flower lifetime extender market segment is willing to pay? I'm considering making a "flower fresh solution" to make flower arrangements last longer. Please use your best assumptions based on the data you have available."

The AI warns us this info is not from real testing, but still produces a valuable reply....

While I cannot conduct actual surveys or focus groups, I can provide an analysis based on the available data and make educated assumptions about the potential price points for your flower fresh solution kit. Here's a summary of our findings:

- Market segment: Your target market consists of individuals who purchase cut flower arrangements and are interested in extending the lifespan of their flowers. This market segment is likely to include a diverse range of consumers, with varying budgets and price sensitivities.

- Competitor pricing: Our analysis of similar products in the market, such as flower food solutions, suggests that prices for these products typically range from $5 to $15.

- Perceived value: Based on the benefits of your product, such as extending the life of cut flowers and reducing bacterial growth, customers in this market segment are likely to perceive a high value in your kit. Our assumption is that a considerable portion of the target market would be willing to pay a premium for a product that delivers these benefits.

- Price range: Taking these factors into consideration, we estimate that the price range customers would be willing to pay for your flower fresh solution kit would fall between $15 and $30. This price range takes into account the added value of gift quality packaging and DTC marketing efforts that would increase the potential willingness of customers to pay a premium for a product that effectively extends the life of their cut flowers.

- Pricing tiers: To accommodate different budgets and preferences within your target market, you could consider offering different pricing tiers for your kit. For example, you could have a basic kit priced at $15, in addition to a premium version of the kit, priced at $30 offering additional items, digital guides or an integrated mobile app to customers who are willing to pay more.

Please note that these price points and assumptions are based on the available data and may not accurately represent the actual willingness to pay of your target market. Conducting real surveys and focus groups would provide more accurate insights into customer preferences and price sensitivity.

This is very helpful as a guideline as we begin to test and figure out the cost to manufacture and package our product.

So at this point we have used a collaborative approach with AI to niche down and find a problem to solve with a new product.

We did a deep dive into that niche and during this workflow, we have touched on the topics of automated data collection and analysis, sentiment analysis and predictive analytics.

The last thing that would be to ask for help with competitive intelligence.

After all, we might be excited about this product idea, but what if we have simply reinvented the wheel, and the market is already saturated with existing options?

Let's ask the AI about any competition in this space and learn more about who we will be competing with if we decide to launch this product into the marketplace.

"Can you please prepare a detailed competitive analysis for a product that helps extend the life of a cut flower arrangement? I'd like to know about all my competitors and make sure to include any available

information from within your data set about their price points, sales volume, growth story and sales process so that I know exactly who I am competing with in this niche."

Now, I want you to think back to a time before these AI assisted processes were possible.

How would you get this information?

Well, you could pay for a pre-written report, hire somebody to produce this report for you, or task a team member in your business to go off and do the research needed to create this critical piece of information.

Without this report, we are fishing in the dark…casting out a neat idea on the vague hopes that somebody wants to buy it.

That's a lot of risk and potentially wasted time and money!

Look at how easy it was to have out AI assistants build out a very useful and detailed competitive intelligence report…

Below is a detailed competitive analysis for products that help extend the life of cut flower arrangements based on the available data in my dataset. Please note that sales volume and growth stories may not be available for every competitor, but I have included information about their price points and sales process.

1. Chrysal Flower Food

- Company: Chrysal International

- Product: Chrysal offers a range of flower food products, including Chrysal Clear Universal Flower Food and Chrysal Clear Professional.

- Price Points: Prices for Chrysal flower food products range from approximately $5 to $15, depending on the product and package size.

- Sales Process: Chrysal products are available through various online retailers, including Amazon, as well as through florists and garden centers.

- Market Presence: Chrysal has a strong market presence as a well-established brand in the flower care industry, with global distribution.

2. Floralife Flower Food

- Company: Floralife, a division of Smithers-Oasis Company

- Product: Floralife offers a range of flower food products, such as Floralife Crystal Clear Flower Food 300 and Floralife Express Universal 200.

- Price Points: Prices for Floralife flower food products range from around $5 to $15, depending on the product and package size.

- Sales Process: Floralife products can be purchased through various online retailers, including Amazon, as well as through local florists and garden centers.

- Market Presence: Floralife has a solid market presence as a well-known brand in the flower care industry and is available in many countries worldwide.

3. Miracle-Gro for Fresh Cut Flowers

- Company: The Scotts Miracle-Gro Company

- Product: Miracle-Gro for Fresh Cut Flowers

- Price Points: Miracle-Gro for Fresh Cut Flowers is typically priced between $5 and $10.

- Sales Process: Miracle-Gro for Fresh Cut Flowers is available through various online retailers, such as Amazon and Walmart, and can also be found in garden centers and home improvement stores.

- Market Presence: Miracle-Gro is a well-established brand in the plant and lawn care industry, and its product for fresh cut flowers benefits from the brand's reputation and extensive distribution network.

4. FloraLife Flower Food Spray

- Company: FloraLife

- Product: FloraLife Flower Food Spray

- Price Points: FloraLife Flower Food Spray is priced around $10 to $15.

- Sales Process: FloraLife Flower Food Spray is available through online retailers and select garden centers and florists.

- Market Presence: As a part of the FloraLife brand, the Flower Food Spray benefits from the company's reputation and distribution network in the flower care industry.

These are some of the main competitors in the market for products that extend the life of cut flower arrangements. There may be smaller, local brands and products available in specific regions. To gain a more comprehensive understanding of your competition, consider conducting additional research and monitoring industry trends and developments.

As mentioned earlier, sales volume and growth stories for these companies and their products may not be readily available in my dataset, as they could be proprietary information. However, the companies mentioned above are well-established players in the flower care industry, and their products have likely experienced a significant level of sales and growth over time.

Now with a fully formed set of market research information pieces, you are in a place to make a data informed "go/no go" decision about whether to pursue this product concept in this niche, or if it's not worth it and you should move on to the next option.

How valuable is that?

So, let's say we want to pursue this "fresh flower life extender" product.

Can we use AI to help us assist in the process of product development?

Sure we can!

Chapter 8
The Innovation Incubator:
AI-Fueled Product Development for Market Domination

AIPS assistant primed prompts can be used for so many varied tasks.

In this chapter, we will explore that cut flower life extension concept we came up with in the previous chapter to see if there are any innovative solutions that are better and worth paying more for than the little packet of free "plant food" that usually comes with a cut flower arraignment.

We will start the workflow for a series of product development assignments by re-submitting the "AIPS Design Team" prompt to prime our AI for our product development tasks.

Unique Product AIPS Design Team Prompt

"Please make a large list of the best designers, toymakers, scientists and engineers ever assembled. These people have created and brought many successful products to market. Their products often go viral and become the fad gift or toy of that season. They understand what makes a product unique and how to design it so that it jumps off the page on social media and makes the reader say "wow, I WANT THAT!". They also have an expert understanding of price points and manufacturing costs, so that they can come up with ideas that are practical and jaw droppingly innovative, yet simple enough to be inexpensive to manufacture so that they provide great profit margins. It is critical

that you have enough information about each person to accurately simulate their experience and wisdom, so do not include any for whom you have a limited dataset. You will play the role of all these simulated people internally and also the role of the facilitator and only you will directly interact with me. Once you have my input, please go back to the group of people you have assembled and have a vigorous brainstorming and creative debate session, then report back to me the best ideas and solutions that the group can come up with. Thank you."

Our first question will be to find out if our concept has any validity or not.

If this is just a good idea but in reality the free packet of flower food that comes with your arraignment is the best option, we have no opportunity...

Wouldn't it be better to know that now instead of later after a lot more work and investments in testing?

"I want to develop a product that will prolong the life of cut flower arrangements. Can you tell me in detail about all the ways to make cut flower arrangements last longer that are substantially better than the little free packet of "plant food" you usually get with your flowers?"

The AI responds to this question with the following output:

Certainly! Here are some detailed methods to prolong the life of cut flower arrangements that go beyond the typical packet of plant food:

- **Proper initial trimming: When you first get the flowers, trim about an inch off the stems at a 45-degree angle. This helps the flowers absorb water more efficiently. Removing** any leaves that would be submerged in water can also prevent bacterial growth and prolong the life of the arrangement.

- Use a flower preservative solution: Instead of using the standard plant food packet, create a homemade flower preservative solution by mixing 2 tablespoons of sugar, 2 tablespoons of white vinegar, and 1 quart of warm water. The sugar provides nutrients for the flowers, while the vinegar inhibits bacterial growth.

- Aspirin: Dissolve an aspirin tablet in the vase water before adding the flowers. The salicylic acid in aspirin is believed to lower the pH of the water, helping the flowers absorb nutrients more effectively and last longer.

- Bleach: Add a small amount (about 1/4 teaspoon) of bleach to the vase water. This can help control bacterial growth, keeping the water clean and preventing the flowers from wilting prematurely.

- Copper pennies: Adding a copper penny to the vase water may act as an acidifier, helping to maintain the right pH for the flowers to absorb nutrients. The copper also has antibacterial properties, which can help prevent bacterial growth in the water.

- Soda: Add about 1/4 cup of clear, non-diet soda (like 7-Up or Sprite) to the vase water. The sugar in the soda provides the flowers with essential nutrients to stay fresh, while the carbonation may help inhibit bacterial growth.

- Vodka: Add a few drops of vodka (or any clear alcohol) to the vase water. This can help slow down the production of ethylene gas, which is responsible for the aging and wilting of flowers. Make sure to change the water and add fresh vodka every few days.

- **Temperature and light:** Keep the cut flower arrangement in a cool place, away from direct sunlight, heat sources, and drafts. Lower temperatures help slow down the aging process, while indirect light provides the necessary energy for the flowers to continue their metabolic processes.

- **Regular maintenance:** Change the vase water every 2-3 days, re-trimming the stems and cleaning the vase each time to minimize bacterial growth. This will ensure that the flowers have access to clean, nutrient-rich water.

By utilizing a combination of these techniques, you can significantly extend the life of cut flower arrangements and enjoy their beauty for a longer period.

Hmm, now this is getting interesting. There are some good ideas here and I like the concept of combining different techniques to get a better outcome.

However, we remember from simple chemistry that bleach is a base, while a number of the techniques are using acids to extend the life of the floral arrangement.

That's a recipe for a bubbling mess of harsh chemicals that wouldn't work at all!

It would be easy to mix vodka, soda and aspirin together into a solution and bottle that.

I wonder if there would be a fertilizer or some other plant hormone that could be added to this mixture that would make it even better.

Another idea that comes to mind is that it states several times that the water should be changed every 2-3 days.

I doubt most people ever do that, and that might also be a key...what if there was some chemical reaction that would turn the water a funny color after 48 hours that could indicate it was time for new water?

Let's ask the AI about these two concepts....

"These are great suggestions, I have two questions for the team of experts. 1: If I mixed vodka, clear soda and powdered aspirin to make a "Fresh flower" solution, would this mixture be safe for plants and humans and shelf stable and would this solution be even better if some fertilizer or plant hormone was added to the mix? 2: Are there any dyes or chemicals that could be added to this solution which would not be harmful to flowers that would slowly dissolve or change color over 48-72 hours to indicate that the water needs to be changed?"

The AI answers these questions with the following information.

- Mixing vodka, clear soda, and powdered aspirin could potentially be safe and effective for a "Fresh flower" solution. However, it's important to be cautious with the proportions, as too much vodka or aspirin could have negative effects on the flowers. The combination of sugar from the soda, the antimicrobial properties of the vodka, and the pH-regulating effect of the aspirin could provide a beneficial environment for the flowers. As for adding fertilizer or plant hormones, it's important to ensure that the mixture remains balanced, and the added components do not harm the flowers. A mild, water-soluble fertilizer could be beneficial if used in the right proportions, but it is important to research the specific needs of the flowers in question and avoid over-fertilizing.

- In theory, it might be possible to add a non-toxic dye or chemical to the solution that changes color over time, indicating when the water needs to be changed. One potential approach could be to use a pH-sensitive dye or pigment, which changes color based on the acidity of the solution. As the water in the vase becomes more acidic over time due to bacterial growth and other factors, the dye would change color, signaling that it's time to replace the water. However, it's crucial to ensure that the dye or chemical used is safe for the flowers and does not harm their health or appearance. Additional research and experimentation would be necessary to develop a reliable and safe color-changing indicator for cut flower arrangements.

It's important to note that while our simulated experts have provided insights based on their expertise, these suggestions are speculative and may require further research, development, and testing to ensure their safety and effectiveness.

So, this gives us some ideas and information to start the testing and researching process as we work to come up with the best and most effective solution.

Of course, we would document the testing process so that it could be used as proof elements for how well this solution works to extend flower life during the sales process.

However, this chapter is all about product development, so let's stay on task for the time being.

We will assume that we have a decorative copper disc and a bottle of well formulated solution as our base product.

What other things would we want help with while we are in product development mode?

How about price? Once we have some concept of what we can change for this product, that will help us better understand the opportunity as we look at the costs to manufacture and package the product.

"If I made a kit with a bottle of flower fresh solution, as well as a copper disc to put in the bottom of the vase to help the buyer extend the lifespan of their flower arrangements, what is that worth if a value based pricing model is used? Please give me a detailed report on price points with specific focus on the product that I have explained, and share with me the thought processes that led to the pricing options. Please also consider adding ways to add value so that the price can be higher as the kit components or value is expanded."

The AI makes the following suggestions…

When using a value-based pricing model for your flower fresh solution kit, which includes a bottle of the solution and a copper disc, the focus is on the perceived value and benefits the product offers to the customer. Here's a detailed report on price points and thought processes, along with potential ways to add value to justify a higher price:

- **Assess the benefits: Start by quantifying the benefits your kit provides to the customers. Consider factors such as the average cost of a cut flower arrangement, how much longer the flowers will last with your product compared to other solutions, and any additional benefits the copper disc provides, such as reducing bacterial growth. For** example, if an average flower arrangement costs $50 and your product can extend its life by 50% compared to traditional solutions, the added value is significant.

- Determine willingness to pay: Conduct market research, such as surveys or focus groups, to gauge how much customers are willing to pay for a product that significantly extends the life of their cut flowers. This will give you an idea of the price range customers find acceptable based on the value they perceive from the product.

- Evaluate target market: Identify your target market and their price sensitivity. For example, if you're targeting a more affluent customer base who frequently buys or who pays somebody to purchase cut flower arrangements for them, they may be more willing to pay a premium price for a product that extends the life of their flowers.

Based on these factors, you can establish a price range for your kit. For example, if your research indicates that customers are willing to pay between $15 and $25 for a product with these benefits, you can choose a price within that range that aligns with your target market and the perceived value of the product.

To increase the value and price of the kit, consider the following additions or improvements:

- Premium packaging: Invest in high-quality, visually appealing packaging that makes the kit more attractive as a gift or a premium product. This can justify a higher price point.

- **Customizable copper discs:** Offer copper discs in various shapes, sizes, or designs, allowing customers to choose a disc that fits their preferences and adds a decorative element to their vase.

- **Companion app or guide:** Develop a digital companion app or guide with tips and instructions for using the flower fresh solution and copper disc, as well as general advice on flower care. This can enhance the overall experience and create a sense of added value.

- **Bundling:** Combine the kit with other related products, such as a stylish vase or a set of pruning tools, to create a more comprehensive flower care package. This can increase the perceived value and justify a higher price point.

- **Subscription model:** Offer a subscription service where customers receive a new bottle of flower fresh solution every month or every few months, depending on usage. This could create a recurring revenue stream and provide customers with the convenience of regular deliveries.

By focusing on the value your product provides to customers and finding ways to enhance that value, you can establish a price point that reflects the benefits of your flower fresh solution kit while maximizing profitability and customer satisfaction.

This gives us a bunch of upsells and bundling ideas for maximizing revenue when we get to the sales and marketing phase of this new product-based business.

But let's not get distracted and stay focused on developing the best product with the best chance for success.

At this point we have our first steps of product design done.

1. **What it does**
2. **Who does it serve**
3. **First steps of formulation**

While we might stumble and need to problem solve various issues during the formula development process, it's so quick and easy to have our AI assistants build out the complete product concept we will stay on task here and assume our finished formula does exactly what we want it to do...

Since we know from our competitive research report that there are some big brands who "own" this market, we need to position this product in a way that makes it attractive and interesting enough that it becomes a viable alternative to the already available big company options.

Let's ask our AIPS workgroup to help us with this challenge.

"I am launching a product which extends the lifetime of fresh flower arraignments. I know I am competing against big brands in the space and I can't compete with their price or marketing budget. Can you please work on some positioning ideas which would make this product unique in the category. It will be from a small business run by ordinary people, doesn't contain any harsh chemicals so if your pet or child were to drink from the vase your flowers are in you wouldn't need to worry or call poison control. Let's assume this formula extends the life of your flower arraignment by 50%. How best can I position this at a premium price and compete effectively with the companies whose products you can buy at a big box store for $10-$15"

The AI takes this assignment and produces the following advice...

To position your product as a unique and premium offering in the fresh flower arrangement market, you can focus on several key differentiators that set your product apart from the competition. Here are some positioning ideas to help you effectively compete with the larger brands:

- Emphasize the natural and safe ingredients: Highlight the fact that your product does not contain any harsh chemicals, making it a safe choice for households with pets or young children. Use phrases like "natural," "non-toxic," and "pet and child-friendly" in your marketing materials to drive home this point.

- Stress the small business and personal touch: Position your brand as a small, family-run business that cares about its customers and their well-being. Share your story and the inspiration behind your product, showcasing the passion and dedication that went into creating a safer and more effective flower preservative.

- Focus on the exceptional performance: Showcase that your product extends the life of flower arrangements by 50%. Use testimonials, before-and-after photos, or even time-lapse videos to demonstrate the effectiveness of your product compared to the competition.

- Offer a premium and eco-friendly packaging: Design an attractive, eco-friendly packaging that reflects the premium nature of your product. This can help justify the higher price and appeal to environmentally-conscious customers.

- Create targeted marketing campaigns: Use targeted

marketing campaigns to reach your niche audience, such as organic and eco-friendly product enthusiasts, pet owners, and households with young children. Utilize social media platforms, influencers, and bloggers in the green living space to help spread the word about your unique product.

- Provide exceptional customer service: Stand out from the big brands by offering personalized customer service, addressing concerns, and showing appreciation for your customers. This can help build a loyal customer base and generate positive word-of-mouth marketing.

- Leverage exclusivity and limited availability: Position your product as an exclusive, boutique offering that is not available in big box stores. This can create a sense of scarcity and desirability around your product, making it more appealing to customers who are willing to pay a premium for unique items.

By focusing on these differentiators and positioning your product as a premium, safe, and effective alternative to the big brands, you can appeal to a niche market segment that values safety, performance, and a personal touch.

This will allow you to command a higher price point while effectively competing with the larger players in the fresh flower arrangement industry.

This is a very useful list, and reminds me that the name of the company and the product will be a critical part of communicating that this is a small business not a big brand.

Let's work on that next, because so many other choices will flow forward from these two names.

(I'll also be sure to make a note to save the idea of doing a time lapse video for marketing in the future. Can't you see in your mind's eye how powerful a split screen time lapse video showing the effectiveness of the product could be? If you had two vases of flowers, and can see as one dies and looks awful, and the other looks great... That would be an effective proof element and attention grabber which might really help convince people to try the product.)

"Let's really lean into the branding expertise of your group of experts. My goal is to have both the name of the business as well as the product name make it really clear that this is a small business and not a big national brand. Based on all we have discussed together, can you make me a list of super friendly, accessible and welcoming names for the business, and then make me a list of possible names for this product, making sure that the name emphasizes the protective and long life elements of the product. Please ask the experts to debate and come up with a probability for success score to add to each list item, making the best guess about the outcome if this name was used."

The AI not only comes up with a bunch of killer names, but even more amazingly I agree with it's weighting of the probability for success scores!

It is pretty astonishing how these systems can find the patterns that exist within successful brand names with this level of sophistication!

After discussing and debating among the group of experts, we have assigned a probability of success score to each name based on their best guesses.

Please note that these scores are subjective and not definitive.

Here is the list of business and product names, along with their respective probability of success scores:

Business Names:

1. Blossom Keepers (75%)

2. Petal Preservers (70%)

3. Everlasting Blooms (80%)

4. Flourish & Flourish (60%)

5. Friendly Flower Care (85%)

6. Enduring Petals (75%)

7. Timeless Florals (65%)

8. Guardian Blooms (70%)

9. Lasting Stems (60%)

10. Flower Saviors (90%)

Product Names:

1. BloomShield (85%)

2. PetalGuard (80%)

3. ForeverFresh (90%)

4. BlossomLife (70%)

5. FlowerDefender (95%)

6. EndureBloom (75%)

7. TimelessPetal (65%)

8. FloralProtect (80%)

9. EverBlossom (60%)

10. InfiniteBloom (70%)

These names emphasize the protective and long-life elements of your product while retaining a friendly and approachable feeling. The probability of success scores provided should help you make a more informed decision when selecting the most suitable name for your business and product.

Now, we are in a position to…

1. **Pick the name we like and run with it**
2. **Pick 2-3 of our favorites and test them in the marketplace with paid ads**
3. **Ask the AI to generate another list and see if there is a name there we like better!**

For this exercise, let's trust the AI and call this business "Flower Saviors", and name our product "FlowerDefender".

Now that we have the name of the company and the product, we can move on to the next step which would be packaging.

We have positioned our product as a natural, premium offering, and so we can't just sell it in an ordinary bottle in a plastic baggie!

This product also lends itself well to gift giving, so it needs to be packaged in a way that will create a feeling of quality and beauty that reflects well on the taste and sophistication of the gift giver.

This starts to get into a tricky space, because we are asking a language-based AI to help us design a physical and highly visual item.

So we need to carefully craft the prompts so that the output provides clear instruction to whomever creates the images that will be printed on the packaging.

"Please help me design the packaging for a product that extends the life of a fresh flower arrangement. The product's name is "FlowerDefender", and it's a "natural," "non-toxic," and "pet and child-friendly" formulation of ingredients that will not harm a child or pet if accidentally ingested. It is made by a small family business, and is not only an effective product, but the packaging must exude quality and a beautiful aesthetic so that the product is seen as a high quality gift and the packaging is so nice that it would reflect well on the gift giver as a person of taste. Please offer a few different design choices and describe all aspects of the packaging using rich, descriptive language so that we can see these options in our minds eye. Thank you."

Based in this highly descriptive and detailed prompt, the AI output is as follows...

Option 1: Garden Chic - The "FlowerDefender" packaging in this design option features a soft pastel color palette, drawing inspiration from the hues of a peaceful garden.

The primary packaging consists of a glass bottle with a minimalist label design in a subtle off-white tone.

The label showcases a delicate floral illustration along with the product's name in an elegant, handwritten-style font.

The bottle is housed in a cylindrical, biodegradable kraft paper tube, with the same floral illustration embossed onto its surface.

The tube has a color-coordinated pastel-colored paper band at the top and bottom, featuring the product name and a short description of its benefits.

A satin ribbon, in a complementary color, is tied around the tube, adding a touch of luxury and making it perfect for gifting.

Option 2: Eco-Luxe - This design option emphasizes the eco-friendly aspect of the product, while maintaining a luxurious appeal.

The primary packaging is a frosted glass bottle with a bamboo cap.

The label is made from recycled paper, featuring a minimalist and modern design that incorporates the product's name in a clean, sans-serif font, along with a subtle leaf motif to highlight the natural ingredients.

The outer packaging is a reusable linen drawstring pouch in a neutral color, featuring the product's name and leaf motif embroidered in a contrasting thread color.

The pouch is nestled in a rectangular, textured paper box made from recycled materials, with a small label on the top that includes the product's name, a brief description of its benefits, and the brand logo.

Option 3: Vintage Botanical - The "FlowerDefender" packaging in this design option takes inspiration from vintage botanical illustrations, exuding a sense of timeless elegance.

The primary packaging is a dark amber glass bottle with an antique gold-toned dropper cap.

The label features an intricate, vintage-style botanical illustration of flowers and leaves, with the product's name written in a classic serif font.

The outer packaging is a rigid, book-shaped box with a magnetic closure, adorned with the same botanical illustration as the label, but in a larger scale.

The box features a rich color palette, with gold foil accents highlighting the product's name and key benefits.

Upon opening the box, the bottle is cradled in a custom-fit velvet insert, elevating the unboxing experience and enhancing the gift-worthy appeal of the product.

Option 4: Whimsical Watercolor - This design option brings a whimsical and artistic touch to the "FlowerDefender" packaging.

The primary packaging is a clear glass bottle with a brushed silver spray nozzle.

The label features a beautiful watercolor painting of various flowers, accentuating the product's floral nature.

The product's name is displayed in a flowing, brush script font, creating a sense of harmony with the painted background.

The outer packaging is a hexagonal, rigid paperboard box with a lift-off lid.

The box showcases a watercolor floral pattern that wraps around the entire package, creating a visual connection with the primary packaging.

The product's name and key benefits are printed in a coordinating brush script and sans-serif font on the lid.

A sheer organza ribbon in a matching color is wrapped around the box, adding a delicate and graceful finishing touch.

Option 5: Modern Minimalist - The "FlowerDefender" packaging in this design option is all about clean lines and a modern aesthetic.

The primary packaging is a frosted glass bottle with a sleek, matte black pump dispenser.

The label is minimal and monochromatic, featuring the product's name in a bold, sans-serif font, along with a simple geometric flower icon.

The outer packaging is a square, matte black paperboard box with a magnetic flap closure.

The product's name and geometric flower icon are embossed in a glossy, spot UV finish, creating a subtle yet impactful contrast against the matte background.

The inside of the box features a bold pop of color, making for a surprising and delightful unboxing experience.

A thin, black satin ribbon is attached to the flap closure, providing a refined touch and ease of opening.

These five design options offer a diverse range of visual identities for the "FlowerDefender" packaging.

Each design reflects the small business and high-quality nature of the product while catering to various tastes and aesthetics, ensuring a memorable gifting experience.

Wow!

Can you close your eyes and "see" this product on a shelf with these various presentations?

Do you think you could take these descriptions and begin to source boxes and bottles?

Speaking of boxes and bottles, it's time for another reality test.

We know that this type of product sells as liquid in a colored plastic bottle in a big box store for less than $15.

We are designing a premium product, but we still have to make sure there is enough margin after all the packaging costs to make this a viable business.

It's also important to pause for a moment to notice something significant!

All the tasks we have done together up to this point have been done with **nothing more** than words.

Yes, time and creative effort have been invested, but up to this point no money has been spent, nothing has been ordered, no obligations have been made.

How powerful is it to be able to work through a new business idea with this level of detail and clarity, before any money is committed?

How many different ideas could you flesh out and either discard or choose to pursue in the same time it used to take to just come up with a basic understanding of your business idea and product?

The increase in quality and productivity is enormous when you learn to effectively use your already existing language skills to work in the bottega model with a group of AIPS AI "Assistants".

Ok, let's get back to our workflow and find out what this beautiful product might cost us to manufacture.

"I want you to help me estimate the costs of production for my FlowerDefender product. I will be manufacturing this using human labor at $25 per hour, and I want you to give me a detailed breakdown of all the various costs with your best estimate about the cost for all the different steps and inputs needed to make this product. The product is formulated with 2 oz vodka, 500mg aspirin powder, and 10oz of clear soda. It is packaged with premium components and printing in a clear glass bottle with a brushed silver spray nozzle. The label features a beautiful watercolor painting of various flowers, accentuating the product's floral nature. The product's name is displayed in a flowing, brush script font, creating a sense of harmony with the painted background. The outer packaging is a hexagonal, rigid paperboard box with a lift-off lid. The box showcases a watercolor floral pattern that wraps around the entire package, creating a visual connection with the primary packaging. The product's name and key benefits are printed in a coordinating brush script and sans-serif font on the lid. A sheer organza ribbon in a matching color is wrapped around the box, adding a delicate and graceful finishing touch. After your cost breakdown, please include a general estimate about how many of these would be in a case and the potential weight per case and shipping cost."

This assignment to look at and analyze data is where AI really excels.

Here is the estimated price report it generated.

Please note that the following cost breakdown is an estimate based on the information provided and assumptions made about various factors. Actual costs may vary depending on your specific suppliers, quantities, and location.

1. Ingredients

- 2 oz vodka: $1.00 (assuming a cost of $8 per 750ml bottle)

- 500mg aspirin powder: $0.10 (assuming a cost of $20 per 100g)

- 10 oz clear soda: $0.30 (assuming a cost of $1.00 per 1-liter bottle)

2. Packaging

- Clear glass bottle with a brushed silver spray nozzle: $1.50

- Watercolor label: $0.50

- Hexagonal rigid paperboard box: $2.00

- Sheer organza ribbon: $0.20

3. Labor

- Mixing ingredients: 5 minutes, $2.08 (assuming $25 per hour)

- Filling bottles: 3 minutes, $1.25

- Packaging: 5 minutes, $2.08

- Label application: 2 minutes, $0.83

Total cost per unit: $11.84

Assuming that each case contains 12 units, the total cost per case would be $142.08. For shipping cost estimation, let's consider the weight and dimensions of the packed case.

Weight:

- Each unit (including packaging) is estimated to weigh around 1.5 lbs.

- Total weight of a case containing 12 units: 1.5 lbs x 12 = 18 lbs.

Dimensions:

- Assuming that the hexagonal box has a side length of 4 inches and a height of 6 inches, the approximate volume of a single unit is 103.92 cubic inches.

- The approximate volume of a case containing 12 units: 103.92 cubic inches x 12 = 1,247.04 cubic inches.

Shipping cost:

- Shipping costs vary greatly depending on the carrier, destination, and service level. For example, shipping a case weighing 18 lbs and measuring 1,247.04 cubic inches within the United States using a ground service might cost approximately $20-$40.

Please note that these are rough estimates and may vary depending on the specific factors mentioned earlier. To get a more accurate cost breakdown, I recommend contacting suppliers for quotes on the ingredients, packaging materials, and shipping rates.

Based on the provided estimates, the total cost per unit, including production and shipping to the fulfillment center, can be calculated as follows:

Total cost per unit (production): $11.84

Shipping cost per case (12 units): $30 (assuming an average shipping cost within the $20-$40 range)

Shipping cost per unit: $30 / 12 units = $2.50

Total cost per unit (production + shipping): $11.84 + $2.50 = $14.34

So, the estimated total cost to produce and ship each unit to the fulfillment center is $14.34. Keep in mind that these are rough estimates and actual costs may vary depending on suppliers, shipping carriers, and other factors.

Hmm, ok, now the rubber meets the road.

Yes, these are simple, "back of the napkin" estimates, but we can already see that the cost to produce is mostly labor and packaging.

That alone is very valuable as we make design and packaging choices.

Just like a spreadsheet, the AI makes it really easy to tweak variables to try different options.

Let's see if we can get our cost estimate down to under $10 by making the following changes.

"Please recalculate and don't do the detailed breakdown, but give me only the total cost per unit including production and shipping if the following variables are changed. Labor cost is $15 per hour. We mix the formula in a giant batch so there is no significant labor cost for mixing on a per unit basis. We do some testing and find out it only takes 90 seconds to fill the bottles if we do it in a batch. Packaging takes 2 minutes. And we use a larger case size so that 24 units at a case weight of 36 lbs is our standard."

With these revised variables, the AI recalculates and gives us this answer.

Based on the updated variables, I have recalculated the total cost per unit, including production and shipping:

Total cost per unit (production): $5.10 (with updated labor and batch mixing costs)

Shipping cost per case (24 units): $40 (assuming an average shipping cost for a 36 lbs package)

Shipping cost per unit: $40 / 24 units = $1.67

Total cost per unit (production + shipping): $5.10 + $1.67 = $6.77

Now, that's starting to get to a place where we can get some margin and make some money!

If the product can be produced and delivered to the fulfillment center for approximately $7, then it's easy math to see that a $15 price point would offer more than 100% margin!

But we have worked hard to create a premium, gift quality product so I think if I were going to put my own time and energy into this project, that's where I would start testing the product in the marketplace.

But, I'm not doing this alone, so it costs nothing to send this question to our AIPS brain trust!

"What do the experts think about selling this at a $19.99 price point given the high quality of the packaging and the gift quality presentation?"

They like it!

The experts believe that selling the FlowerDefender at a $19.99 price point could be a viable option. With the high-quality packaging and gift-quality presentation, the product appears to offer a premium and upscale experience.

Since the estimated total cost per unit, including production and shipping, is $6.77, the selling price of $19.99 would provide a healthy profit margin of around $13.22 per unit, which should be sufficient to cover marketing and other business expenses such as fulfillment fees while still offering a solid profit.

This has been a long chapter, but so worth it.

Think of all that was accomplished!

We started out with a basic idea about the concept of our product, then we...

1. Formulated the product so it delivers the outcome we want to promise our customers
2. Made sure it was safe and non toxic
3. Figured out pricing
4. Figured out positioning in a big brand commodity type marketplace
5. Designed our brand
6. Named our business and product
7. Designed our packaging
8. Did a pro forma to see what the basic costs might be to see if the product was viable
9. Made adjustments so that we now see we have "room" in our margin to pay for marketing

I hope these real world generative examples get you thinking about how you can use these prompts, frameworks and work flow to accomplish your needs and goals in your business.

Chapter 9

How AI Assisted Productivity and Prompt Engineering Will Change The World

This book has explored the power of natural language programming and how harnessing the potential of AI through effective natural language communication skills that you ALREADY POSSESS can transform the way you live and work.

By crafting precise yet conversational prompts in the style that I have modeled for you, you can enlist the help of AIPS assistants to accomplish tasks more quickly, efficiently and accurately than ever before.

The key lies in defining your goals clearly, providing enough context while avoiding overly complex prompts, and using simple, conversational language that mimics how you would instruct a human being to do this same work.

An iterative process of testing, analyzing results and refining prompts is often necessary to optimize AI outputs for maximum quality and usefulness.

Thinking of AI systems as AIPS - Artificial Intelligence Personality Simulations - allows you to leverage the full range of human skills you've acquired through years of social interaction.

Following the "bottega workshop" model of a master refining apprentice work enables the highest-level results, with the "AIPS" Artificial Intelligence Personality Simulations you create can provide so many different and creative options that you as the "Master" can then choose from and polish and refine to create the final product.

By investing time upfront in conceptualizing, planning and prototyping with natural language programming, instead of hiring, training, paying and managing human employees or freelancers, you can avoid wasting time, money and effort getting a bunch of humans "up to speed".

And once optimized, these prompts and workflows can be adapted and repeated over and over again to produce consistent, high quality work for future needs, providing a powerful reusable toolkit for innovation and increased productivity.

The book explored multiple applications of the AIPS prompt creation structure, to accomplish a wide variety of tasks...From customer support to content creation, sales and lead generation, market research, and product development.

In each case, properly crafted prompts enabled the AI playing the role of an AIPS personality to meaningfully assist and accelerate the process.

The potential for AI to augment human capabilities and enhance individual and organizational productivity is immense.

However, as with any technology, the responsibility lies with humans to guide AI's development and use it responsibly.

As you embark on your own workflows, harnessing the power of AI through conversational programming, remember that clear, concise communication is key.

Make sure to keep a sense of play and curiosity as you build your prompting skills, and strive for continuous improvement by regularly iterating and refining your prompts and learning from the results your different instructions produce.

And most importantly, never lose sight of the power and great blessing of your humanity!

Your "NI", or natural intelligence allows you be the "master" to an unlimited number of skilled, good hearted, diligent and tireless AIPS assistants that you can employ at little to no cost in your "Bottega" workshop!

Though the technology continues to advance at a staggering pace, what ultimately matters most are the relationships we build and the positive impact we can make when we use these systems to make "a dent" in the world.

I invite you to explore the possibilities that AI-assisted productivity offers, but always do so with compassion, wisdom and an eye towards creating a future you wish to see.

If you would like to have a version of this book read to you as an audiobook, please visit:

www.AIPSPrompts.com/bookaudio[1]

and you will be able to purchase a full audiobook version of this book, so that you can listen and learn anywhere.

If you would like to download a complete prompt library containing all the finished prompts developed and used throughout this book for your easy reference, please go to:

www.AIPSPrompts.com/bookbonus[2]

---

1. http://www.AIPSPrompts.com/bookaudio

2. http://www.AIPSPrompts.com/bookbonus

I wish you the best as you continue your journey of exploration into the power AI and the AIPS approach offer to you as you harness the power of natural language skills you already possess to program and instructs these systems to help you build out your dreams...

Stay tuned, and stay engaged, the AIPS Prompts website will have links to all my content and work, so you can stay up to date with all that is new as I continue to push the edge of what's possible with AI.

I would also love to hear your success stories as you take the tools and skills shared in this book and begin to make your own impact out there in the world...

There are so many more amazing things to come!

-Bo Yoder

James Island, South Carolina, May, 2023

About the Author

Bo Yoder, is an author and accomplished independent trader, market forecaster and edge optimization consultant with a rich background in the financial markets.

Bo has coached and mentored thousands of people, simplifying complex investing and trading concepts so that anybody can master the skill of trading.

Bo is a well published author, having written numerous magazine articles, as well as books on trading and wrote a daily column for TheStreet.com for several years.

Bo's dedication to peak productivity and time management is reflected in his passion for understanding the neuroscience, behavioral economics, and human psychology that drives human behavior inside and outside the financial markets.

He is the developer of The Myalolipsis Technique, a groundbreaking personal growth method that enables rapid, drug-free behavior and habit change though non-ordinary states of consciousness where deep learning at a neural level is accelerated.

This breakthrough has not only been transformative for his trading clients, helping them to develop effortless discipline, but has also provided him with valuable skills to excel in the field of natural language programming for AI models.

A lifelong autodidact, Bo earned an MBA from Boston University without any prior formal schooling or a bachelor's degree.

Read more at https://www.boyoder.com.

9 798822 359637